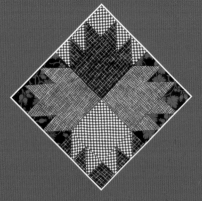

# Tried
## *and*
# True

# Tried
## *and* True

### New Quilts from
### Favorite Blocks

SANDY BONSIB

*Martingale*®
& COMPANY

## CREDITS

President: Nancy J. Martin
CEO: Daniel J. Martin
VP and General Manager: Tom Wierzbicki
Publisher: Jane Hamada
Editorial Director: Mary V. Green
Managing Editor: Tina Cook
Technical Editor: Darra Williamson
Copy Editor: Liz McGehee
Design Director: Stan Green
Illustrator: Laurel Strand
Cover and Text Designer: Regina Girard
Photographer: Brent Kane

That Patchwork Place® is an imprint
of Martingale & Company®.

Tried and True: New Quilts from Favorite Blocks
© 2005 by Sandy Bonsib

Martingale & Company
20205 144th Avenue NE
Woodinville, WA 98072-8478 USA
www.martingale-pub.com

Printed in China
10 09 08 07 06 05        8 7 6 5 4 3 2 1

The information in this book is presented in good faith, but no warranty is given nor results guaranteed. Since Martingale & Company has no control over choice of materials or procedures, the company assumes no responsibility for the use of this information.

## MISSION STATEMENT
*Dedicated to providing quality products
and service to inspire creativity.*

**Library of Congress Cataloging-in-Publication Data**
Bonsib, Sandy.
   Tried and true : new quilts from favorite blocks / Sandy Bonsib.
      p. cm.
   ISBN 1-56477-602-6
   1. Patchwork—Patterns. 2. Quilting. 3. Patchwork quilts. I. Title.
   TT835.B62826  2005
   746.46'041—dc22

2004023946

## DEDICATION

This book is dedicated to my students. Many of these quilts were made with blocks I created as class samples to demonstrate a particular technique, so it seems very appropriate to dedicate this book to the wonderful ladies (and sometimes men) for whom these blocks were created. I have learned so much from you. You have enriched my life beyond measure. I have laughed with you and sometimes felt like crying with you as you have shared stories of your lives—and thus pieces of yourselves. You are why I do what I do, and you are my inspiration to continue. Thank you from the bottom of my heart.

## ACKNOWLEDGMENTS

Thank you, first and foremost, to my husband, John Bickley, who helped me with so many tasks as I created the quilts that became part of this book. He made dinners, took care of animals, did laundry, and yes, even ironed clothes so I could follow my passion to create with fabric. To say that I couldn't do this without him is completely true.

Thank you to Kathy Staley and Becky Kraus, both extremely talented machine quilters. Their ideas and beautiful workmanship bring my quilts to life and help them last a lifetime.

Thank you to Lynn Ahlers and Rachel Vanderlaan for contributing their quilts to this book. I am proud to include their beautiful, inspiring, and awesome work.

Thank you to Darra Williamson, my editor. It has been a pleasure to work with her; her expertise, hard work, and positive attitude are wonderful.

And, finally, thank you to Martingale & Company for once again (the sixth time!) believing in me.

# Contents

*Easy blocks,*
*Easy piecing, and*
*Easy techniques for combining blocks*

=

*A new look,*
*A complex look,*
*A surprisingly different look*

*But—so easy to do!*

Traditional blocks are just that—blocks that have become a part of our history because they have been used by generations of quilters. Traditional blocks are our heritage as well as our inspiration. Making traditional blocks is one of my favorite things to do. Creating a new look with them is even more exciting.

Most quilters come from a traditional (as opposed to an art) background. They make quilts because they love them, because their grandmothers and mothers made them, because they want to carry on a family tradition. Traditional blocks have withstood the test of time. They are popular and appealing, and their construction is not complex. This book features the very blocks that many of us learned in a beginning quiltmaking class—but they don't look like basic blocks unless you look closely. The techniques used to create "new" blocks from these old favorites are surprisingly easy.

As a teacher who teaches basic quiltmaking classes over and over again, I find myself with many single blocks created for classroom demonstrations. How many Rail Fence quilts does a person need—or want? Thinking that there must be something I could do with these blocks to use them up, I began to experiment. I was soon amazed with the wonderful new looks I could get for the blocks I loved—and with very little effort.

Another thing that amazed me was how the colors in these sample blocks coordinated to make attractive quilts. When I choose fabrics for a class demonstration, I often choose "not-my-favorite" fabrics and make no effort to match colors with previously made blocks. Often I am choosing fabrics in the last hour before I need to leave for class, so coordinating, matching, and using these blocks in the same quilt is the last thing on my mind. How surprised I was to discover how mismatching worked in my favor as I put the quilts in this book together. I think these quilts are reminiscent of something my grandmother would have made from her scrap bag. Wow—all those years of agonizing over fabric choices only to find I can get great quilts without all that agony!

Traditional blocks highlighted in this book include Rail Fence, Churn Dash, Pinwheel, Flying Geese, Nine Patch Variation, Four Patch, Bear's Paw, Star Variation, Kaleidoscope, and Album Patch—the same basic blocks often taught to first-time quilters. The construction of these blocks isn't difficult. It is, therefore, easy for you to begin a quilt from this book. Using these blocks to create new blocks and a new look adds an unexpected twist. The blocks often appear more complex than they really are.

I hope this book provides new quilters with ideas for using their newfound knowledge and experience in interesting, often surprising ways. I also hope that experienced quilters who love traditional blocks will add their own touches to these quilts that honor our heritage with a creative flair. Finally, no matter what your level of skill, I hope you always remember that making quilts should always be fun.

Create! Be inspired! Enjoy!

*I am frequently asked by my students how I come up with ideas for my quilts. To be creative, most of us need to start with something we know. It is then easier to go outside our comfort zone because we feel we are on firm footing to begin with. Creating something new from something familiar is where I started for this book.*

## GENERATING IDEAS

First of all, get rid of ideas that limit your creativity. For example: Blocks are square, right? But must they be? Can they be rectangular? Yes!

Many settings for our blocks are traditional and predictable. They are illustrated in the same familiar ways in most quilt books. But settings can be unusual, can't they? Yes! How about a spiral setting instead of rows?

And fabrics need to match, right? No! Did your grandmother's fabrics match in her quilts? No! And didn't she make beautiful quilts? Yes!

The following are ideas I used to create quilts in this book.

## PLAY WITH YOUR BLOCKS

The first design idea is a simple one. Just play with your blocks!

1. Start with a single block.

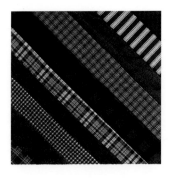

2. Fold it in half on the diagonal . . .

. . . or fold it in half vertically or horizontally. Look intriguing?

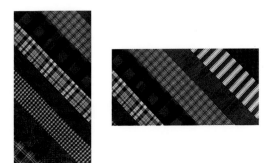

3. Cut a square the same size as the block.

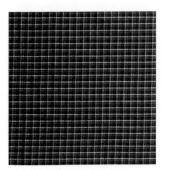

4. Place the two right sides together and fold the block back on the diagonal. (This is what I did for "Flying Geese Fandango Spiral" on page 70.)

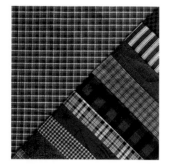

Or, fold the block back vertically or horizontally. Look better?

5. Take two blocks that are the same pattern but made up in different colors. Place them right sides together and fold one back on the diagonal. (This is what I did for "Rail Fence Riot" on page 67.)

Or fold one back vertically or horizontally. (This is what I did for "Album Patch Ambiance" on page 37.)

Or fold one back vertically or horizontally and slightly "whopper-jawed" or askew. (Lynn Ahlers did this in "Nine Patch Nuance" on page 47.)

What do you think?

## GIVE YOUR BLOCK A TWIST

Turn on point a block that isn't traditionally set that way. I did this in "Kaleidoscope Kaper" (page 32).

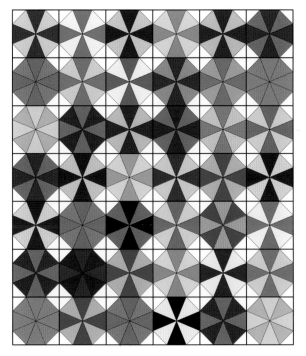

*Traditional setting for Kaleidoscope blocks*

*My setting for Kaleidoscope blocks*

## TRY A DIFFERENT SETTING

Try a unique setting, such as in "Flying Geese Fandango Spiral" (page 70), in which the blocks radiate from the center in a circular pattern rather than march in horizontal or diagonal rows.

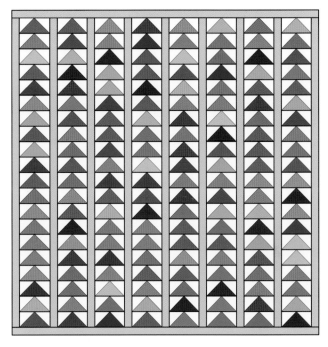

*Traditional setting for Flying Geese*

*My setting for Flying Geese*

## RECOMBINE ELEMENTS OF A BLOCK

Take parts of a block—not the whole block—and combine them to make a new block. That's what I did in "Bear's Paw Bonanza" (page 62).

*Traditional Bear's Paw block*

*My Bear's Paw block*

## ALTERNATE BLOCKS OF DIFFERENT SIZES

Take blocks of different sizes and alternate them, making the smaller block the same size as the larger one with the addition of a fabric strip or two, as in "Four Patch Fun and Churn Dash Chuckle" (page 42).

## ARRANGE TRADITIONAL SHAPES IN NONTRADITIONAL PATTERNS

Play with traditional shapes (such as triangles) and traditional motifs (such as stars, outlined below in red) and arrange them to make recognizable but nontraditional patterns. This is what Rachel Vanderlaan did to create "Sierra's Sunshine and Stars" (page 74).

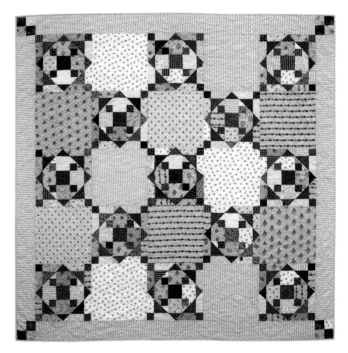

*Eight-pointed star*

## FINISH A FEW BLOCKS WITH BORDERS

Take a few blocks and add a border—or two, or three, or four—rather than making more blocks to enlarge the quilt. This works especially well if you are pressed for time or if you have run out of fabric for the blocks!

*By adding multiple borders, you can turn just a few blocks into a large quilt.*

## INCORPORATE BLOCKS INTO THE BORDERS

Remember that blocks are not just for the quilt top but can be a part of the quilt's borders, too. Change just the background fabric to indicate where the top ends and the border begins.

*Make a "border" by changing the background fabric.*

*In the following pages you'll find the basic information you need for choosing and cutting the fabrics, sewing the blocks, and assembling the quilt tops for all the projects in this book. I've included lots of illustrations—and some "tried-and-true" tips—to guide you as well.*

## FABRIC AND COLOR SELECTION

Use colors you like in your quilts. You have to live with your quilts, so you should like them! If you like a quilt pattern in this book, but not the colors I've chosen, make the quilt in any colors you choose.

No matter how many fabrics and colors you choose for your quilt, make sure you create contrast. Most quilts look better when some fabrics are light in value, some are dark, and others are medium. If you don't have a full range of values, you need to be more careful in creating contrast. Always remember to judge lightness or darkness from a distance—that means 10 feet or more away. We see most of our quilts from across the room, either on a wall or a bed. The only time we're really up close and personal with our fabric is when we buy it, cut it, or sew it. For the rest of its life, we see it from a distance, as part of a quilt, so that's the basis on which we need to make our choices.

Don't worry about matching colors and patterns. Quilts are much more interesting if their colors aren't perfectly matched. I learned this lesson well as I created the quilts for this book using blocks intended only as class samples. And our grandmothers certainly couldn't match either colors or patterns all of the time, but they still created wonderfully charming quilts. It's the mismatching that makes their quilts so interesting.

When in doubt, make a sample. I often make a sample to be sure I understand how to make the blocks or to check that I've done the math correctly. If the sample doesn't turn out quite as planned, it often becomes a label on the back of my quilt.

Use a design wall when you are ready to arrange the blocks for your quilt. You can make a design wall by temporarily attaching a piece of extra-thick fleece to the wall. The blocks stick to the fleece without the use of pins or other fasteners. Since it's a vertical surface, all of the blocks are the same distance from your eyes. (When you lay your blocks out on the floor or another horizontal surface, some blocks are closer to you and some are farther away.) A vertical surface gives you a better perspective, and you can decide more easily if your blocks are visually balanced.

Allow yourself the freedom to change your mind. If the border fabric you were planning to use doesn't look good when you get your blocks sewn together, don't feel you must use it just because you bought it. It won't look any better after it's sewn into the quilt. Often you can use that fabric on the back of the quilt (meaning you won't have to buy as much backing fabric), in pillows to go with the quilt, or in another project. Don't force something that doesn't work.

As you work on your quilt, keep in mind that you know more than you think you know. You may not have gone to art school (most quilters haven't), but you've been looking at color, design, and balance since you were old enough to notice. You just may not have the art words for these concepts. Trust your gut feelings!

# ROTARY CUTTING

Directions for the quilts in this book are for rotary cutting all pieces, and all measurements include a ¼"-wide seam allowance. The blade on a rotary cutter is very sharp. Keep it away from children and remember to use the safety guard after every cut.

## Cutting Strips, Squares, and Rectangles

Instructions are for cutting right-handed. Reverse the instructions if you are left-handed.

1. Fold the fabric, wrong sides together, aligning the crosswise and lengthwise grains as much as possible. Smooth the fabric to flatten it. The selvages probably will not line up. Sometimes they will be very skewed. Don't worry about that. Place the fabric on the cutting mat with the folded edge closest to you.

2. Align a square ruler along the folded edge of the fabric. Place a 24"-long ruler to the left of the square, just covering the uneven raw edges of the fabric. Remove the square ruler and cut along the right-hand edge of the long ruler, rolling the rotary cutter away from you. Discard this first strip, which is called the cleanup cut.

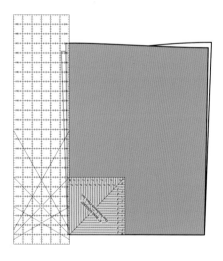

3. To cut strips, align the required measurements on the ruler with the newly cut edge of fabric. For example, to cut a 2½"-wide strip, place the 2½" mark of the ruler on the edge of the fabric.

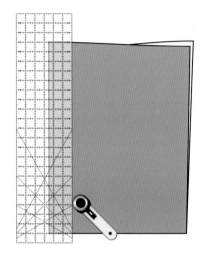

4. To cut squares and rectangles, cut strips in the required widths. Remove the selvage ends of the strip. Then align the required measurement on the ruler with the left edge of the strip and cut the square or rectangle. Continue cutting until you have the required number of pieces.

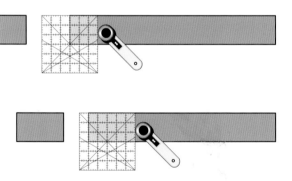

5. For some quilts, you will cut strips, sew them together into strip sets, and then cut segments from the strip sets. First, trim the end of a strip set to square it up (this is your cleanup cut). Then align the required measurement on the ruler with the left edge of the strip set and cut the specified number of segments.

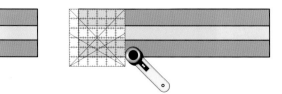

## Cutting Triangles

Two different types of triangles are used for the quilts in this book. The difference between them is the direction of the straight grain. On half-square triangles, the straight grain is on the two short sides. On quarter-square triangles, the straight grain is on the long, diagonal side.

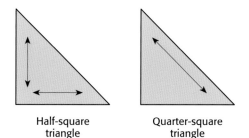

Half-square triangle          Quarter-square triangle

For half-square triangles, cut a square the size given in the quilt instructions. Cut the square once diagonally.

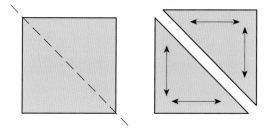

For quarter-square triangles, cut a square the size given in the quilt instructions. Cut the square once diagonally but do not move either piece; line up the ruler on the opposite diagonal and cut again.

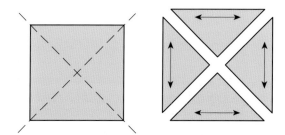

## PIECING

The single most important thing when making quilts is to maintain a consistent ¼"-wide seam allowance as you piece. Otherwise, your block will not be the desired finished size. If that happens, the size of everything else in the quilt is affected, including alternate blocks, sashing, and borders. Measurements for all components of the quilt are based on blocks that finish to the desired size plus ¼" all around for the seams.

### Creating an Accurate Seam Guide

It is important to establish an exact ¼"-wide seam guide on your sewing machine. Some machines have a special ¼" foot, which allows you to use the edge of the foot to guide the edge of the fabric for a perfect ¼"-wide seam.

If your machine does not have such a foot, don't despair! You can easily create a seam guide with masking tape or electrical tape. Electrical tape is available in different colors that contrast with the color of your machine, making the tape easy to see.

Place a ruler under the presser foot. Gently lower the needle onto the first ¼" marking from the right-hand edge of the ruler. Place a piece of tape along the right-hand edge of the ruler, in front of the needle, as shown.

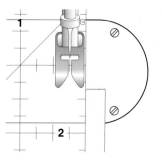

Sew a test seam using your new guide to make sure your seams are ¼" wide; if they are not, readjust the seam guide. Many quilters find that they need to take a scant ¼" seam rather than a full ¼" to get their blocks the right size.

## Piecing Half-Square-Triangle Units

I use two methods to make half-square-triangle units. Both enable me to avoid sewing the triangles on their bias edges.

### Sew and Flip

Cut squares the size given in the quilt instructions. Pair two squares right sides together and draw a diagonal line on the wrong side of the lighter square. Stitch on the drawn line. Flip one triangle over so the right side is visible and press. Carefully trim the seam allowance to ¼". Each pair of squares yields one half-square-triangle unit.

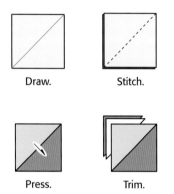

Draw.     Stitch.

Press.     Trim.

I use a similar sew-and-flip method to create flying-geese units and star points with two squares and a rectangle. Draw a diagonal line on the wrong side of one square. Position the square on the rectangle and sew on the diagonal line. Trim the seam allowance to ¼" and press the triangle toward the corner of the unit. Repeat with the remaining square.

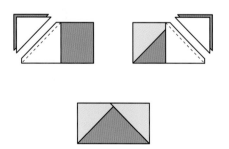

**TIP**

To make sewing half-square-triangle units easier, position tape in front of and behind the presser foot on your sewing machine, aligning one edge of the tape with the needle. Be careful not to cover the feed dogs. As you sew, follow the edge of the tape with the corners of the square. You won't need to draw a diagonal line on the square.

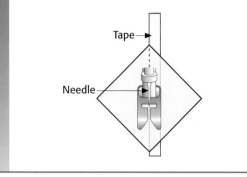

Tape→

Needle→

### Two for One

Cut squares the size given in the quilt instructions. Pair two squares right sides together and draw a diagonal line on the wrong side of the lighter square. This is not your sewing line; it will become your cutting line. Draw another set of lines ¼" from the drawn line. These are your sewing lines. (You don't need to draw these sewing lines if your machine has a ¼" presser foot.) Stitch on the second set of drawn lines or ¼" from the centerline on both sides. Cut on the centerline. Press each unit open, with the seam allowances toward the darker fabric. Each pair of squares yields two half-square-triangle units. I often make these units slightly larger than required and then trim them to the size needed.

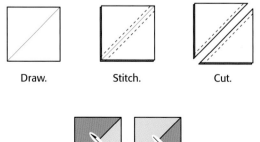

Draw.     Stitch.     Cut.

Press.

## PINNING

Take the time to pin pieces together when assembling blocks. There is a tendency for the pieces to shift slightly as you feed them under the presser foot. A few carefully placed pins will keep this shifting to a minimum. I sew right over the pins, removing them after I've stitched a seam. Although I was cautioned many years ago that I'd break needles that way, that very seldom happens to me. If you prefer, you can remove pins as you come to them.

## PRESSING

I use a steam iron on a cotton setting to press seams and finished blocks. While steam can cause some distortion, I use it because the resulting seams and blocks are nice and flat. Just be sure to press carefully in an up-and-down motion; don't drag the iron over the pieces.

Press seams to one side, usually toward the darker of the two fabrics. Pressing arrows are provided in illustrations when the direction in which you press the seams is important. Following these arrows will make constructing the blocks and assembling the quilt top easier.

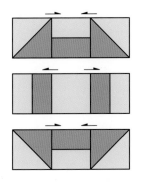

## BIAS-TUBE LETTERS

Quilts sometimes convey a message through sayings or words; for an example, see "Nine Patch Nuance" on page 47. There are a number of ways to add lettering to your quilts. One of my favorite methods is bias-tube appliqué.

Bias-tube letters are easy to make and fun to play with. I use bias bars to make my letters. The bars I use are metal and come in a variety of widths. I use the ½" width most often.

1. For ½" finished bias tubes, cut bias strips 1⅜" wide. Fold the strips lengthwise, wrong sides together, and sew along the long edge, using a ⅛" seam allowance. Slide the bar into the tube, rotate the seam so it is in the center of the bar, and press.

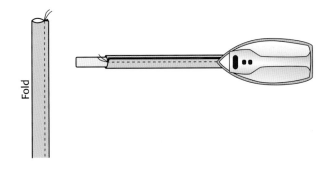

Fold

When I have been unable to find my bias bars, I have rotated the seam and pressed the bias tube without a bar.

2. Draw the letters on your quilt top with light-colored chalk. (It's easy to remove if you don't press too hard.) Attach the bias tubes to the quilt top with a glue stick, overlapping the ends. I like that "slightly frayed" look so I generally don't turn the ends of the tubes under, but you can turn them under if you prefer a more finished appearance. Allow the glue to dry.

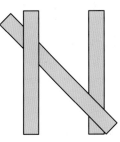

3. Using size 8 pearl cotton and a size 24 chenille needle, sew a running stitch down the center of each bias tube to secure it.

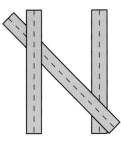

Appliqué the edges of tight curves using regular thread. I use a back whipstitch. This stitch is similar to a slip stitch, except the needle is inserted into the background fabric just a few threads *behind* the spot where the thread comes out of the appliqué shape.

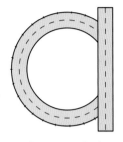

Appliqué curved edges.

## SQUARING UP THE BLOCKS

No matter how carefully you sew, some blocks may end up a little smaller or a little larger than the desired size. Trying to sew different-size blocks together can be very frustrating. Trimming the blocks to the same size—squaring them up— before joining them makes sewing them together much easier.

For example, perhaps the blocks in your quilt are designed to be 10½" (including seam allowances). Before you sew the blocks together, measure each block. If the difference is fairly insignificant— some of your blocks are 10¼" and some as large as 10¾"—you will be able to ease them together, and you won't need to square up the blocks. But if the difference between the smallest and largest blocks is greater than ½", you'll need to square up the blocks. With smaller blocks, such as 6½" blocks, the difference between the smallest and largest needs to be ¼" or less. Otherwise you'll need to square up these too.

Determine which block is the smallest and trim the other blocks to match. Although you may not reduce the block size significantly, the change will affect the sashing strips and borders. For example, if some of the blocks are as small as 10", you'll want to cut all of the blocks down to 10". If your quilt includes sashing strips, you'll need to cut these down to fit the 10" blocks. You'll need to make similar adjustments to the borders as well.

Use a rotary cutter and a square ruler to trim the blocks. The important thing to remember is that you need to remove equal amounts from all sides of the block. If you are trimming a 10½" block down to 10", you need to remove ¼" from all four sides. If you are starting with a 10¼" block, you need to remove ⅛" from all four sides.

**Caution:** If triangle points come to the edge of your finished block, be careful not to trim away the seam allowance. You don't want to lose those triangle points when you sew the trimmed block to another block or piece of fabric.

## ASSEMBLING THE QUILT TOP

When you have made all the blocks and cut all the remaining pieces, it's time to put them all together to make the quilt top.

Arrange the blocks on your design wall, following the directions and illustrations provided with each quilt. Do you have too many lights, brights, or dark fabrics in the same area? Is a particularly eye-catching color or pattern distributed evenly throughout the quilt?

For straight-set quilts, join the blocks in horizontal rows. Press the seams in opposite directions from row to row so opposing seams will butt up against each other when you join the rows. Pressing arrows are provided to show you the ideal pressing direction for the seams. Join the rows, making sure to match the seams between the blocks. Secure each seam with a pin if desired.

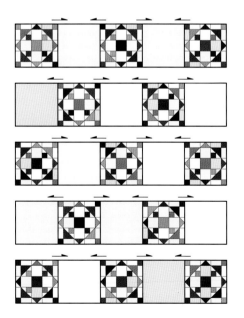

For diagonally set quilts, refer to the quilt photo and diagrams to arrange and sew the blocks in diagonal rows. Add the side triangles. Join the diagonal rows and add the corner triangles last.

For diagonally set quilts, I cut the side and corner triangles larger than necessary and then trim the edges to straighten them after I've sewn the rows together. I do this for two reasons. First, oversized triangles create "float," which is an area between the block points and the first border. It creates the illusion that the blocks are "floating" on the background. Second, when the blocks float, I don't need to worry about stitching off the corners of the blocks when I add the borders.

To create the float and straighten the quilt edges, you will need to trim all four sides of the completed quilt top. To do this, place a long ruler on the block points at the measurement specified in the quilt directions, and trim the excess fabric with a rotary cutter. In the example shown below, the ruler is positioned with its 1½" marking on the block points. When the excess fabric is trimmed and the first border is added, there will be a float of 1¼" between the corners of the block and the border.

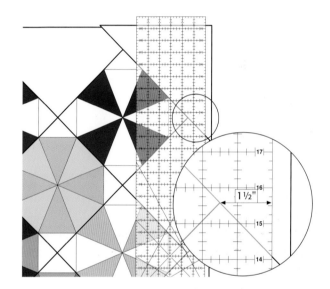

*You thought you were almost done, didn't you? But now that you've made the quilt top, it's time to finish the quilt. Do you want to add borders? Many times our grandmothers did not. If it is necessary to piece the quilt backing (and it usually is), how do you do it? How do you choose a batting? Do you machine or hand quilt— or do you have someone else do the quilting for you? How do you make and apply a binding? And don't forget to make a label. The following pages tell you how.*

## ADDING BORDERS

You will see borders with and without corner squares on the quilts in this book. Some quilts don't even have borders. Borders are not an absolute requirement. If you like your quilt without them, eliminate them. If you want to make your quilt larger, especially to fit a bed, adding additional borders or making borders wider than the pattern specifies can easily accomplish that.

The most fabric-efficient way to cut borders is on the crosswise grain, which means across the width of the fabric. Since many quilts are longer than a strip of fabric cut on the crosswise grain, you may need to piece two or more strips together to create one long enough for the edge of your quilt. When piecing border strips, I prefer to use a diagonal seam.

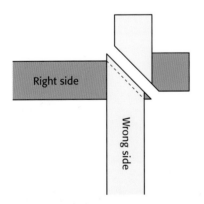

Right side

Wrong side

I'll sometimes cut border strips on the lengthwise grain so I won't need to piece them. If you prefer to cut borders from the lengthwise grain, you'll need to purchase more fabric

for your border. You'll need enough to equal the longest measurement of your quilt and then some. For example, if a quilt measures 55" x 75", I purchase 84" (2⅓ yards) of fabric. This allows me to cut long borders without piecing them and also allows for shrinkage, which could be 4" to 6" with this length of fabric.

It's important to measure and cut border strips to fit your quilt. Cutting long strips, sewing them to the quilt top, and then trimming the excess often results in a quilt with wavy borders. Also, the measurement along the edges of a quilt may differ slightly from the measurement through the center due to stretching that occurs during construction. This is normal, so measure through the center of the quilt, not along the edges, when figuring border lengths.

Specific measurements are provided for cutting the border strips for each quilt. These measurements are based on blocks sewn with accurate ¼"-wide seam allowances. Measure your blocks to be sure they are the correct size. To be safe, measure your quilt top through the center after the blocks are sewn together to determine the correct border lengths.

### Borders without Corner Squares

Most of the projects in this book do not use corner squares. If the quilt directions call for corner squares and you prefer not to use them, be sure to purchase extra yardage and to add the necessary length to the border strips before you cut.

1. Measure the length of the quilt top through the center. Cut two border strips to that measurement. Mark the center points of the quilt edges and the border strips with a pin. If you wish, you can also mark the quarter points.

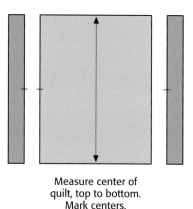

Measure center of
quilt, top to bottom.
Mark centers.

2. Pin the borders to the sides of the quilt top, matching the pins and the ends and easing as necessary. Sew the borders to the quilt. Press the seams toward the border.

3. Measure the width of the quilt top through the center, including the side borders just added. Cut two border strips to that measurement. Mark, pin, and sew the borders to the top and bottom of the quilt as described in the previous steps. Press the seams toward the border.

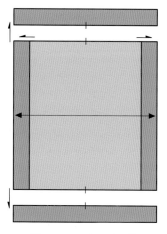

Measure center of quilt,
side to side, including
borders. Mark centers.

## Borders with Corner Squares

Corner squares give you the opportunity to use another color or fabric in the border. You will use shorter border strips for this type of border because you are adding corner squares to complete the length.

1. Measure the width and length of the quilt top through the center. Cut two border strips to each measurement.

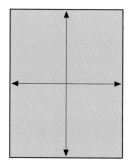

Mark the center points of the quilt edges and the border strips with a pin. If you wish, you can also mark the quarter points.

2. Pin the side borders to opposite sides of the quilt, matching the pins and the ends and easing as necessary. Sew the borders to the quilt. Press the seams toward the border.

3. Sew a corner square to each end of the remaining border strips. Press the seams toward the strip. Pin the borders to the top and bottom of the quilt, matching the pins, seams, and ends, and easing as necessary. Sew the borders to the quilt. Press the seams toward the border.

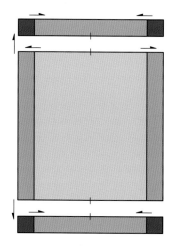

## BACKING

Choosing backing fabrics can be fun. You can repeat a fabric you've used on the front of the quilt, or you can choose a different fabric that coordinates with the front.

Cut the backing so that it is 4" to 6" longer and wider than the quilt top. This allows for any shifting of the layers that may occur during quilting and for the slight shrinkage that occurs when the layers are quilted. You'll need to piece the backings for most of the quilts in this book in order to have a large-enough piece. Unless I've noted otherwise, place the backing so the seam runs vertically. Sometimes, when it means using less fabric, I've indicated running the seam horizontally instead.

If the quilt top is just a few inches too wide for a single width of backing fabric, I often add a strip down the middle of the backing. The strip can be a single piece of fabric, or it can be pieced from left-over blocks, squares, and rectangles.

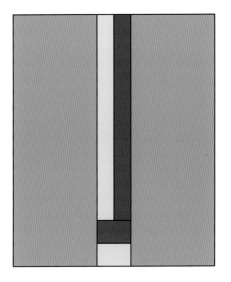

### *Piecing the Backing from Leftovers*

Instead of buying fabric, consider piecing the backing from larger pieces of fabric left over from the front of the quilt. Cut the leftover fabrics into strips or squares. Sew them together randomly or in an interesting pattern until you have a backing piece of the required size. If you have leftover blocks from the front, these can be pieced into the back as well.

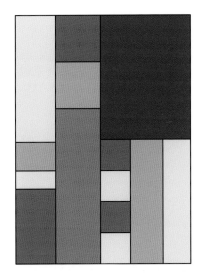

## BATTING

You have many batting choices. Polyester and cotton battings are the most widely used. I prefer cotton battings for my quilts. Cotton battings are flat, easy to quilt, and heavier in weight than polyester, helping wall quilts to hang well. Cotton battings are also denser than polyester battings, so I choose a thin one if I want to hand quilt. If you prefer a puffier batting, choose a medium- or low-loft polyester.

Cotton battings now come in a range of lofts, just as polyester ones do. For thinner battings, my favorite is Quilters Dream Cotton. "Request" is the thinnest and "Select" is just a little thicker. For thicker cotton battings, my favorite is Warm & Natural. I do not preshrink my cotton battings. The unlaundered batting shrinks slightly when I wash my quilt for the first time. This makes my quilt look like my grandmother's quilts and I like that look. As with the backing, the batting should be cut 4" to 6" larger than the quilt top.

## MAKING THE QUILT SANDWICH

The quilt sandwich is made up of the quilt top, batting, and backing. Place the backing, wrong side up, on a large table. Use masking tape to anchor the backing to the table. Make sure the backing is flat and wrinkle-free, but be careful not to stretch it out of shape. Place the batting on top of the backing, smoothing it well. Center the pressed quilt top, right side up, on top of the batting. Smooth out any wrinkles. Baste with safety pins if you are machine quilting, or thread if you are hand quilting. If you are using pins, do not place them in the areas you intend to quilt.

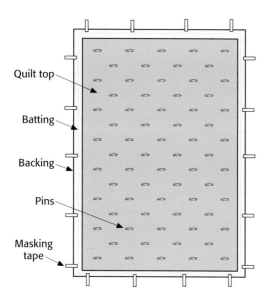

Quilt top

Batting

Backing

Pins

Masking tape

If you are taking your quilt to a professional machine quilter (an increasingly popular option), you will not need to make the quilt sandwich. You will take your quilt top and quilt backing (seamed if necessary) to the quilter. You may be able to purchase the batting directly from the quilter at less than the retail cost because she (or he) will only charge you for what your quilt needs. When you buy a packaged batting, you often must buy a larger piece than you need, which results in leftover pieces.

## QUILTING

Whether you quilt your quilts or someone else does it for you, there are many ways to quilt and many designs from which to choose. Choosing from all your options is often more difficult than doing the quilting—or at least it can seem so. You can machine quilt, hand quilt, or have someone else machine or hand quilt for you. You can use regular quilting thread, use decorative threads, or even use pearl cotton. You can match the quilting thread to the fabrics, or choose not to.

### Machine Quilting

Quilting straight lines is perhaps the easiest way to quilt, especially if you are doing it yourself and are new to machine quilting.

You'll need a walking foot to help feed the quilt layers through the machine without causing them to shift or pucker. The Pfaff sewing machine has a built-in walking foot, called a dual feed, that I love. Other machines require a separate attachment.

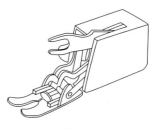

Walking foot

Use straight-line quilting to stitch straight lines, to outline a geometric shape, or to quilt in the ditch (in the seam).

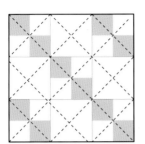

Diagonal straight lines

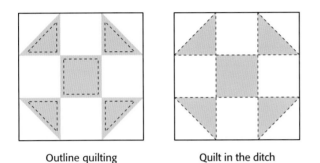

Outline quilting          Quilt in the ditch

For free-motion quilting, you guide the fabric in the direction you want it to go. You will need a darning foot and the ability to drop the feed dogs on your sewing machine. Free-motion quilting requires some practice. Make sure you take the time to machine quilt some samples before you start quilting on your quilt.

The most common method of free-motion quilting is stippling, but free-motion quilting can also be used to outline a motif in the fabric, or create loops, hearts, and many other designs.

Pearl cotton can be used for machine quilting. Use a Schmetz Topstitch needle (130N) in size 100/16 for number 8 pearl cotton and in size 80/12 for number 12 pearl cotton. See Maurine Noble's book *Machine Quilting Made Easy* (Martingale &

Company, 1994) for more information on machine quilting.

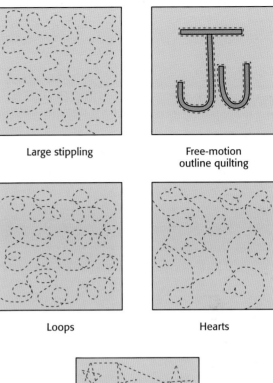

Large stippling          Free-motion outline quilting

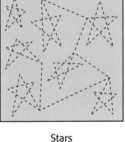

Loops          Hearts

Stars

## Hand Quilting

Hand quilting takes longer to do than machine quilting, but if you like handwork, you may prefer to hand quilt. Generally, quilters thread-baste quilts for hand quilting. Then they use hand-quilting thread and a needle called a Between to make the quilting stitches. As with machine quilting, stitching ¼" away from seam lines or stitching around pieced or appliquéd shapes is an easy option. Pearl cotton can be used for hand quilting if you like the folk-art look. Use number 8 pearl cotton and a size 24 chenille needle. You won't be able to load your needle with stitches like you can with traditional hand quilting, and your stitches will be larger than regular quilting stitches, but this type of quilting adds a homey feeling to your quilts.

## BINDING

I prefer a double-fold, straight-grain binding. I use a double-fold, bias binding only when I want to show off a striped or plaid fabric. Bias binding requires more fabric than straight-grain binding. In the quilt directions, I have indicated when I used bias binding. If you don't see the word *bias*, cut the binding on the straight grain.

1. For straight-grain binding, cut the required number of 2"-wide strips across the width of the fabric. You will need enough strips to go around the outside edge of the quilt plus extra for the folded corners. Piece the strips together on the diagonal. Press the seams open.

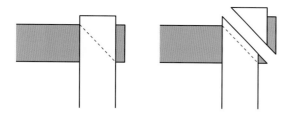

2. Cut one end of the pieced strip at a 45° angle. Don't measure; just eyeball it. Fold about ¼" of the angled edge to the wrong side and press. Then press the entire strip, wrong sides together.

3. Trim the excess backing and the batting even with the edges of the quilt top.

4. Begin on a straight edge of the quilt, away from a corner. Align the raw edges of the binding with the raw edges of the quilt. Begin stitching approximately 3" from the angled end of the binding strip, using a ¼"-wide seam. Backstitch at the beginning for added strength.

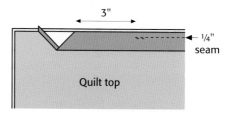

5. When you get close to the first corner, insert a pin ¼" from the edge of the quilt. (Again, just eyeball it). Sew up to the pin and backstitch. Remove the pin from the quilt and the quilt from the machine.

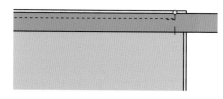

6. Fold the binding up, away from the quilt; then back down onto itself. Align the fold of the binding along the edge you just stitched, and the raw edges of the binding with the raw edge of the adjacent side of the quilt. Begin stitching at the edge of the folded binding (and the quilt top), *not* ¼" in. Be careful not to fold over the corner of the backing fabric.

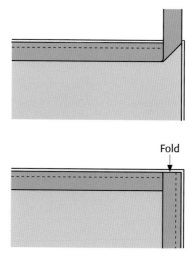

7. Continue sewing the binding to the quilt, turning and stitching all four corners as described in step 6. When you get close to the point at which you started, insert the tail of the binding strip inside the angled starting end, trimming the tail if it is too long. Finish sewing the binding to the quilt, stitching a little past the place where you began.

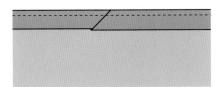

8. Fold the binding to the back of the quilt. Sew the binding to the back with a slip stitch, using thread to match the binding. A natural miter will form at the corners on the front of the quilt. On the back, fold the binding to form a miter.

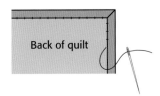

Back of quilt

## ADDING A LABEL

It is important to label your quilts. This can be done simply and quickly. If the backing fabric is light in color, use a fine-point permanent marker (size .05 or .08) to write directly on the back of your quilt. I stitch the binding first; then I use it as a straight edge to guide my writing. If you need or want to make a separate label, choose a simple shape, such as a heart, and write (or stitch, if you prefer) your name, city, state, and the date (usually just the year) you finished your quilt. Stitch your label to the back of the quilt.

The most important thing about a label is to just do it. In future years, you'll be glad you did. How many of us have a family quilt with no information about who made it, or where, or when? A label that tells something about the quilt adds to its value, both monetarily and sentimentally.

By Sandy Bonsib, 53½" x 62". Machine quilted by Becky Kraus.

## FABRIC REQUIREMENTS AND SUPPLIES

"Kaleidoscope Kaper" is a scrappy quilt and you can include a wide variety of prints, plaids, stripes, and checks in the fabric mix. With so many different fabrics, it is difficult to tell you the exact number of fabrics, the amount of any one fabric, and the exact total you will need. When an *assortment* is indicated, the amount given is only a guideline. You can mix ¼-yard cuts (9" x 42"), fat quarters (18" x 21"), ⅛-yard cuts, and large scraps, depending upon how scrappy you want *your* quilt to be. You may work with fabric from your existing fabric collection, with fabric purchased just for this quilt, or with a combination of the two. You may wish to add fabrics as you go along. If you are purchasing ¼-yard cuts, fat quarters, or ⅛-yard cuts, you will be purchasing more than the totals listed in order to have more variety to choose from. Read through all the instructions before you begin.

## MATERIALS

*Yardage is based on 42"-wide fabric. Fabrics for piecing are listed from largest to smallest quantity.*

3½ yards *total* of assorted red, orange, green, blue, and purple fabrics in medium-light, medium, medium-dark, and dark values for blocks

3 yards of muslin for blocks, side and corner triangles, and binding

3½ yards of fabric for backing (horizontal seam)

60" x 68" piece of batting

Template plastic

## CUTTING

*Measurements include ¼"-wide seam allowances. Cut strips from the crosswise grain of the fabric.*

**From the assorted red, orange, green, blue, and purple fabrics, cut a *total* of:**

122 rectangles, 3⅞" x 10"

**From the muslin, cut:**

22 rectangles, 3⅞" x 10"

10 strips, 2⅝" x 42"; crosscut into 144 squares, 2⅝" x 2⅝". Cut each square in half on the diagonal to make 288 half-square triangles.

6 squares, 11½" x 11½". Cut each square in half on both diagonals to make 24 quarter-square side triangles. You will have 2 triangles left over.

2 squares, 7½" x 7½". Cut each square in half on the diagonal to make 4 half-square corner triangles.

6 strips, 2" x 42", for binding

## MAKING THE QUILT

Refer to "Basic Quiltmaking Techniques" (pages 17–23) and "Finishing the Quilt" (pages 25–31) as needed. You will make a total of 72 Kaleidoscope blocks: 22 blocks that combine a colored fabric and muslin and 50 blocks that combine two colored fabrics. Choose fabrics that contrast for most of the blocks. The finished blocks measure 6" x 6" in the quilt (6½" x 6½" unfinished).

1. Trace the pattern on page 36 onto template plastic. Cut out the template and check it for accuracy by placing the template on the original. Adjust the template or recut it if necessary.

2. Fold each 3⅞" x 10" colored rectangle in half as shown, right or wrong sides together. Trace the template on each folded rectangle and cut to make four triangles. You will have a total of 488 large triangles in matching sets of four.

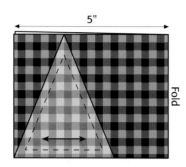

Trace.

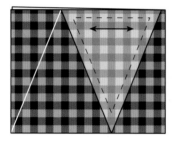

Turn to nest.
Cut to make 4 triangles.

3. Repeat step 2, using the 3⅞" x 10" muslin rectangles. You will have 88 large triangles in sets of four.

4. Select two sets of colored triangles from step 2. Sew one triangle of each fabric together as shown. Press the seams toward the darker fabric. Make four matching units for each block (200 units total).

Make 4.

5. Sew two matching units from step 4 in pairs as shown; press. Sew the pairs together; press. Trim all dog-ears. Make 50.

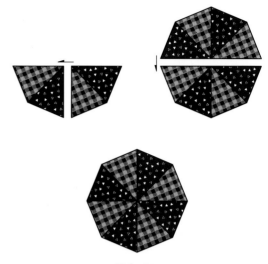

Make 50.

6. Repeat steps 4 and 5, pairing a remaining set of colored triangles with a set of muslin triangles. Make 22.

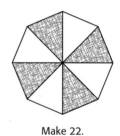

Make 22.

7. Sew a 2⅝" muslin triangle to the lighter colored or muslin triangles in each unit from steps 5 and 6 as shown; press.

 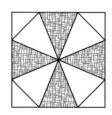

Make 50.          Make 22.

## ASSEMBLING THE QUILT

1. Arrange the blocks on point in diagonal rows as shown in the quilt diagram below. Place the colored/muslin blocks on the outside edges. Place the remaining blocks as desired, balancing bright colors and eye-catching patterns. Place the muslin side and corner triangles.

2. Sew the blocks and side triangles in diagonal rows. Press the seams in alternating directions from row to row. Sew the rows together; press. Add the corner triangles last, pressing the seams toward the corner triangles.

Quilt diagram

3. Trim the edges of the quilt top 2½" from the points of the dark triangles in the blocks as shown.

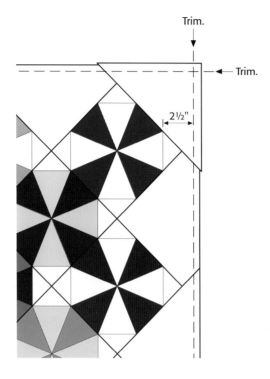

4. Layer the quilt top with batting and backing; baste. Quilt as desired. Circular quilting patterns highlight the circular contour of the Kaleidoscope blocks. Use the 2"-wide muslin strips to bind the quilt edges, and label your quilt.

*Detail of circular quilting pattern on "Kaleidoscope Kaper"*

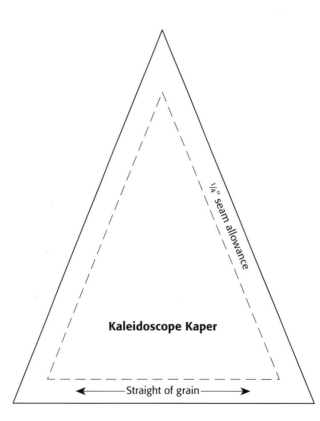

¼" seam allowance

**Kaleidoscope Kaper**

←—— Straight of grain ——→

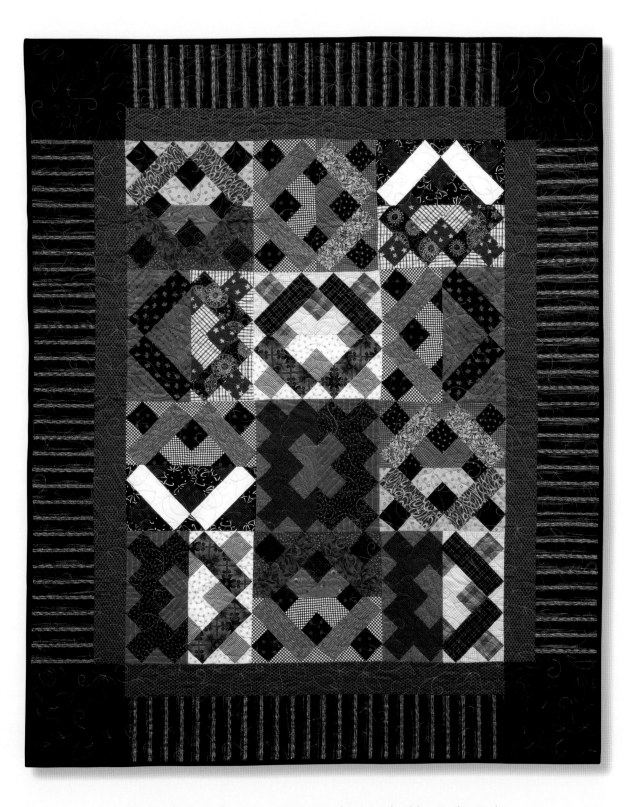

By Sandy Bonsib, 54" x 65½". Machine quilted by Kathy Staley.

Album Patch Ambiance

## Fabric Requirements and Supplies

"Album Patch Ambiance" is a scrappy quilt and you can include a wide variety of prints, plaids, stripes, and checks in the fabric mix. With so many different fabrics, it is difficult to tell you the exact number of fabrics, the amount of any one fabric, and the exact total you will need. When an *assortment* is indicated, the amount given is only a guideline. You can mix ¼-yard cuts (9" x 42"), fat quarters (18" x 21"), ⅛-yard cuts, and large scraps, depending upon how scrappy you want *your* quilt to be. You may work with fabric from your existing fabric collection, with fabric purchased just for this quilt, or with a combination of the two. You may wish to add fabrics as you go along. If you are purchasing ¼-yard cuts, fat quarters, or ⅛-yard cuts, you will be purchasing more than the totals listed in order to have more variety to choose from. Read through all the instructions before you begin.

## Materials

*Yardage is based on 42"-wide fabric. Fabrics for piecing are listed from largest to smallest quantity.*

2 yards *total* of assorted fabrics for blocks (fabric A)

1⅛ yards of black stripe for outer border

1 yard *total* of assorted fabrics for blocks (fabric B)

1 yard *total* of assorted fabrics for blocks (fabric C)

⅝ yard of dark gray fabric for inner border

⅜ yard of black fabric for corner blocks

½ yard of black fabric for binding

3½ yards of fabric for backing (horizontal seam)

60" x 72" piece of batting

## Cutting

*Measurements include ¼"-wide seam allowances. Cut strips from the crosswise grain of the fabric.*

**From the assorted A fabrics, cut a *total* of\*:**

48 squares, 2⅝" x 2⅝", in matching sets of 4. Cut 2 squares from each set in half on the diagonal to make 48 half-square corner triangles.

12 rectangles, 2⅝" x 6⅞"

36 squares, 4½" x 4½", in matching sets of 3. Cut each square in half on both diagonals to make 144 quarter-square side triangles.

**From the assorted B fabrics, cut a *total* of:**

48 rectangles, 2⅝" x 6⅞", in matching sets of 4

**From the assorted C fabrics, cut a *total* of:**

96 squares, 2⅝" x 2⅝", in matching sets of 8

**From the dark gray fabric, cut:**

5 strips, 3½" x 42"

**From the black stripe, cut:**

5 strips, 6½" x 42"

**From the black fabric, cut:**

4 squares, 9½" x 9½"

**From the black binding fabric, cut:**

7 strips, 2" x 42"

*\*Cut four 2⅝" squares, one 2⅝" x 6⅞" rectangle, and three 4½" squares from the same fabric.*

# MAKING THE QUILT

Refer to "Basic Quiltmaking Techniques" (pages 17–23) and "Finishing the Quilt" (pages 25–31) as needed. You will make 12 Album Patch blocks. Each block uses three fabrics: one each of fabrics A, B, and C. Refer to the block diagram as needed. The finished blocks measure 11½" x 12" in the quilt (12" x 12½" unfinished). Instructions are for one block.

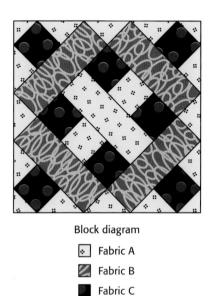

Block diagram

⊡ Fabric A

▧ Fabric B

■ Fabric C

1. Sew matching 2⅝" fabric C squares to opposite sides of a 2⅝" fabric A square as shown; press. Make two.

Make 2.

2. Sew step 1 units to opposite sides of a matching 2⅝" x 6⅞" fabric A rectangle as shown; press.

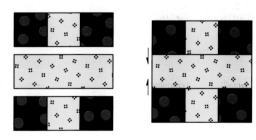

3. Sew matching 2⅝" x 6⅞" fabric B rectangles to opposite sides of the unit from step 2 as shown; press.

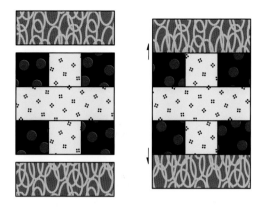

4. Sew matching fabric A quarter-square side triangles to opposite ends of a remaining 2⅝" x 6⅞" fabric B rectangle as shown; press. Trim the dog-ears. Make two.

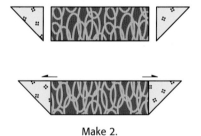

Make 2.

5. Sew matching fabric A quarter-square side triangles to opposite sides of a 2⅝" fabric C square as shown; press. Make four.

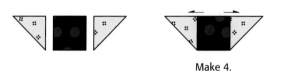

Make 4.

6. Sew two units from step 5 to the unit from step 3 as shown; press.

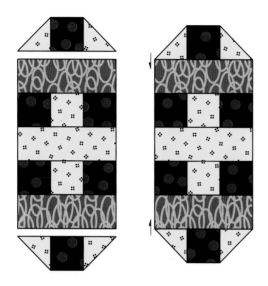

7. Sew a remaining unit from step 5 to a unit from step 4 as shown; press. Make two.

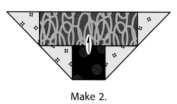

Make 2.

8. Sew the units from step 7 to the unit from step 6 as shown; press. Sew matching fabric A half-square corner triangles to each of the four corners; press. Trim the dog-ears.

9. Carefully trim the block ¼" beyond the points as shown.

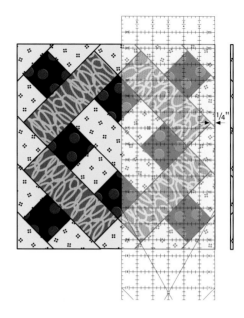

10. Repeat steps 1–9 to make a total of 12 Album Patch blocks.

11. Cut each Album Patch block in half vertically, mix them up, and sew two different halves together. Blocks should measure 12" x 12½".

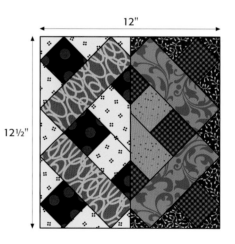

## ASSEMBLING THE QUILT

1. Arrange the blocks in four horizontal rows of three blocks each, turning the blocks so the center seam alternates vertically and horizontally as shown in the quilt diagram below

2. Sew the blocks together into rows. (You will need to ease the blocks a bit to fit since they are slightly different sizes.) Press the seams in alternating directions from row to row.

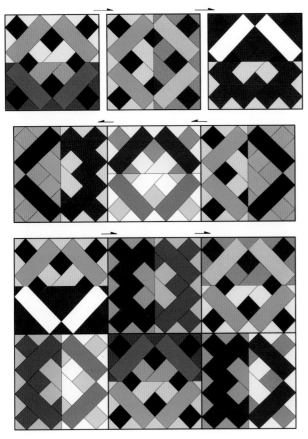

Quilt diagram

3. Sew the rows together; press.

4. Trim two 3½"-wide dark gray strips to 3½" x 36" for the top and bottom borders. Sew the remaining 3½"-wide strips together end to end to form one long strip. From this strip, cut two 3½" x 47½" strips for the side borders.

5. Repeat step 4 using the 6½"-wide black stripe strips.

6. Sew a 36"-long dark gray strip to a 36"-long black stripe strip to make a border unit. Press the seams toward the black strip. Make two. Repeat to sew 47½"-long dark gray and black strips together; press. Make two.

7. Sew a 47½"-long border unit to the sides of the quilt top. Press the seam toward the dark gray border.

8. Sew a 9½" black corner square to opposite ends of each 36"-long border unit. Press the seams toward the border unit. Sew the borders to the top and bottom of the quilt top; press.

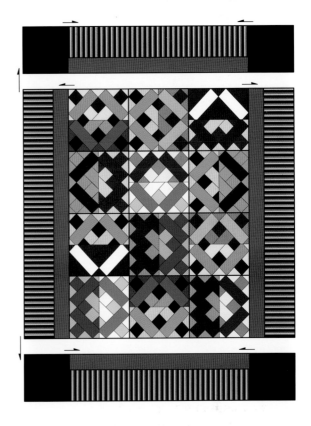

9. Layer the quilt top with batting and backing; baste. Quilt as desired. Use the 2"-wide black strips to bind the quilt edges, and label your quilt.

By Sandy Bonsib, 94⅜" x 107⅝". Machine quilted by Kathy Staley.

## FABRIC REQUIREMENTS AND SUPPLIES

"Four Patch Fun and Churn Dash Chuckle" is a scrappy quilt and you can include a wide variety of prints, plaids, stripes, and checks in the fabric mix. With so many different fabrics, it is difficult to tell you the exact number of fabrics, the amount of any one fabric, and the exact total you will need. When an *assortment* is indicated, the amount given is only a guideline. You can mix ¼-yard cuts (9" x 42"), fat quarters (18" x 21"), ⅛-yard cuts, and large scraps, depending upon how scrappy you want your quilt to be. You may work with fabric from your existing fabric collection, with fabric purchased specifically for this quilt, or with a combination of the two. You may wish to add fabrics as you go along. If you are purchasing ¼-yard cuts, fat quarters, or ⅛-yard cuts, you will be purchasing more than the totals listed in order to have more variety to choose from. Read through all the instructions before you begin.

## MATERIALS

*Yardage is based on 42"-wide fabric. Fabrics for piecing are listed from largest to smallest quantity.*

3 yards of large-scale plaid for border

3 yards *total* of assorted fabrics for Churn Dash blocks (fabric A)

3 yards *total* of assorted fabrics for Churn Dash blocks (fabric B)

3 yards *total* of assorted fabrics for Four Patch blocks

2 yards of black stripe for side and corner triangles

1½ yards of red-orange fabric for Four Patch blocks

1⅛ yards of blue-and-green fabric for Four Patch block A

1⅛ yards of blue fabric for Four Patch block B

¾ yard gold fabric for binding

8½ yards of fabric for backing (horizontal seams)

101" x 114" piece of batting

## CUTTING

*Measurements include ¼"-wide seam allowances. Cut strips from the crosswise grain of the fabric unless noted otherwise.*

**From the assorted A fabrics, cut a *total* of*:**

48 squares, 3" x 3"

96 squares, 3⅜" x 3⅜", in matching pairs; cut each square in half on the diagonal to make 192 half-square triangles in matching sets of 4

192 rectangles, 1¾" x 3", in matching sets of 4

*\*Cut one 3" square, two 3⅜" squares, and four 1¾" x 3" rectangles from the same fabric.*

**From the assorted B fabrics, cut a *total* of**:**

96 squares, 3⅜" x 3⅜", in matching pairs; cut each square in half on the diagonal to make 192 half-square triangles in matching sets of 4

192 rectangles, 1¾" x 3", in matching sets of 4

*\*\*Cut two 3⅜" squares and four 1¾" x 3" rectangles from the same fabric.*

**From the assorted Four Patch block fabrics, cut a *total* of:**

252 squares, 2½" x 2½", in matching pairs

**From the red-orange fabric, cut:**

37 strips, 1¼" x 42"; crosscut into:
    126 rectangles, 1¼" x 4½"
    126 rectangles, 1¼" x 6"

**From the blue-and-green fabric, cut:**

24 strips, 1½" x 42"; crosscut into:
    64 rectangles, 1½" x 6"
    64 rectangles, 1½" x 8"

**From the blue fabric, cut:**

24 strips, 1½" x 42"; crosscut into:
    62 rectangles, 1½" x 6"
    62 rectangles, 1½" x 8"

**From the black stripe, cut:**

7 squares, 15" x 15". Cut each square in half on both diagonals to make 28 quarter-square side triangles.

2 squares, 10" x 10". Cut each square in half on the diagonal to make 4 half-square corner triangles.

**From the *lengthwise* grain of the large-scale plaid, cut:**

2 strips, 8½" x 99⅛"

2 strips, 4¾" x 93⅞"

**From the gold fabric, cut:**

11 strips, 2" x 42"

## MAKING THE QUILT

Refer to "Basic Quiltmaking Techniques" (pages 17–23) and "Finishing the Quilt" (pages 25–31) as needed.

### *Making the Churn Dash Blocks*

You will make 48 Churn Dash blocks. Each block is made from two contrasting fabrics: one each of fabric A and fabric B. Refer to the block diagram as needed. The finished blocks measure 7½" x 7½" in the quilt (8" x 8" unfinished). Instructions are for one block.

Block diagram
■ Fabric A
▦ Fabric B

1. Sew one fabric A half-square triangle and one fabric B half-square triangle together to make a half-square-triangle unit. Press the seams toward the darker fabric. Make four matching units.

Make 4.

2. Using the same two fabrics, sew one 1¾" x 3" fabric A rectangle to one 1¾" x 3" fabric B rectangle as shown. Press the seams toward the darker fabric. Make four matching units.

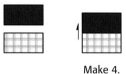

Make 4.

3. Arrange the half-square-triangle units from step 1, the units from step 2, and the matching 3" fabric A square as shown. Sew the square and units together in rows; press. Sew the rows together; press.

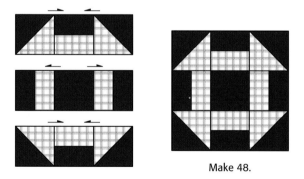

Make 48.

4. Repeat steps 1–3 to make a total of 48 Churn Dash blocks in a variety of fabrics.

## Making the Four Patch Blocks

You will make 63 Four Patch blocks. The center four-patch unit in each block is made from two contrasting fabrics and each block is surrounded by a frame of red-orange strips. Then the blocks are divided: Four Patch block A is finished with a frame of blue-and-green strips and Four Patch block B is finished with a frame of blue strips. The finished blocks measure 7½" x 7½" in the quilt (8" x 8" unfinished).

1. Sew two contrasting 2½" squares together as shown. Press the seams toward the darker square. Make two matching units. Arrange and sew the units together as shown; press. Make a total of 63 four-patch units in a variety of fabrics.

Make 63.

2. Sew a 1¼" x 4½" red-orange rectangle to opposite sides of each four-patch unit as shown; press. Sew a 1¼" x 6" red-orange strip to the remaining sides of the unit; press. Make 63.

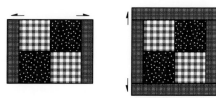

Make 63.

3. Sew a 1½" x 6" blue-and-green strip to opposite sides of a four-patch unit from step 2; press. Sew a 1½" x 8" blue-and-green strip to the remaining sides of the unit; press. Make 32 and label them Four Patch block A.

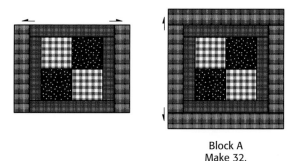

Block A
Make 32.

4. Sew a 1½" x 6" blue strip to opposite sides of each remaining four-patch unit from step 2; press. Sew a 1½" x 8" blue strip to the remaining sides of the unit; press. Make 31 and label them Four Patch block B.

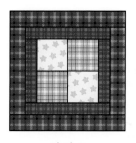

Block B
Make 31.

## ASSEMBLING THE QUILT

1. Turn the Churn Dash and Four Patch A and B blocks and arrange them in horizontal on-point rows as shown in the quilt diagram below. Make nine rows of seven Four Patch blocks and eight rows of six Churn Dash blocks, alternating the rows as shown. Place the black stripe side and corner triangles.

Quilt diagram

2. Sew the blocks and side triangles together in diagonal rows. Press the seams toward the Four Patch blocks. Sew the rows together; press. Add the corner triangles last, pressing the seams toward the corner triangles.

3. Trim the edges of the quilt top 2" from the corner of the Four Patch blocks as shown.

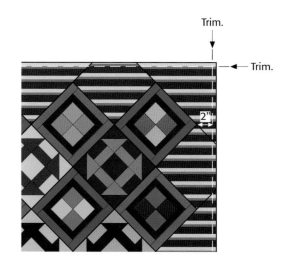

4. Refer to "Adding Borders" on page 25. Mark, pin, and sew the 8½" x 99⅛" borders to the sides of the quilt. Press the seams toward the borders. Repeat to mark, pin, and sew the 4¾" x 93⅞" borders to the top and bottom of the quilt; press.

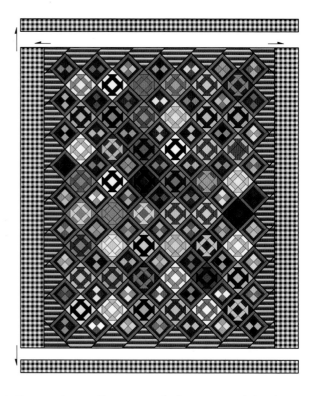

5. Layer the quilt top with batting and backing; baste. Quilt as desired. Use the 2"-wide gold strips to bind the quilt edges, and label your quilt.

By Lynn Ahlers, 72½" x 66½". Machine quilted by Kathy Staley.

## FABRIC REQUIREMENTS AND SUPPLIES

"Nine Patch Nuance" is a scrappy quilt and you can include a wide variety of prints, plaids, stripes, and checks in the fabric mix. With so many different fabrics, it is difficult to tell you the exact number of fabrics, the amount of any one fabric, and the exact total you will need. When an *assortment* is indicated, the amount given is only a guideline. You can mix ¼-yard cuts (9" x 42"), fat quarters (18" x 21"), ⅛-yard cuts, and large scraps, depending upon how scrappy you want *your* quilt to be. You may work with fabric from your existing fabric collection, with fabric purchased specifically for this quilt, or with a combination of the two. You may wish to add fabrics as you go along. If you are purchasing ¼-yard cuts, fat quarters, or ⅛-yard cuts, you will be purchasing more than the totals listed in order to have more variety to choose from. Read through all the instructions before you begin.

## MATERIALS

*Yardage is based on 42"-wide fabric. Fabrics for piecing are listed from largest to smallest quantity.*

5 yards *total* of assorted fabrics for blocks (fabric A)

1⅞ yards of blue fabric for letter background

1¼ yards of red fabric for letters

1 yard *total* of assorted fabrics for blocks (fabric B)

⅝ yard of bluish green fabric for binding

4 yards of fabric for backing

79" x 72" piece of batting

Glue stick

6½" x 6½" square ruler (optional but helpful)

## CUTTING

*Measurements include ¼"-wide seam allowances. Cut strips from the crosswise grain of the fabric unless noted otherwise.*

**From the assorted A fabrics, cut a *total* of*:**

204 squares, 3" x 3", in matching pairs

204 rectangles, 3" x 8", in matching pairs

**From the assorted B fabrics, cut a *total* of:**

102 squares, 3" x 3"

**From the *lengthwise grain* of the blue fabric, cut:**

1 strip, 18½" x 60½"

**From the bluish green fabric, cut:**

8 strips, 2" x 42"

*\*Cut two 3" squares and two 3" x 8" rectangles from the same fabric.*

## MAKING THE QUILT

Refer to "Basic Quiltmaking Techniques" (pages 17–23) and "Finishing the Quilt" (pages 25–31) as needed.

### Making the Nine Patch Variation Blocks

You will make 102 Nine Patch Variation blocks. Each block is made from two contrasting fabrics: one each of fabric A and fabric B. The finished blocks measure 6" x 6" in the quilt (6½" x 6½" unfinished). Instructions are for one block.

1. Sew matching 3" fabric A squares to opposite sides of a 3" fabric B square as shown; press.

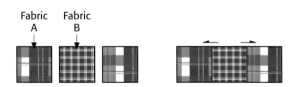

2. Sew matching fabric A rectangles to opposite sides of the unit from step 1 as shown; press.

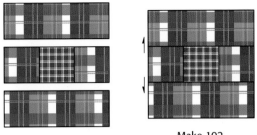

Make 102.

3. Repeat steps 1 and 2 to make a total of 102 Nine Patch Variation blocks in a variety of fabrics.

4. Layer two blocks right sides up with the seams running in the same direction. Use your rotary cutter and ruler to cut the blocks in half *slightly* at an angle as shown.

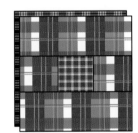

OR

5. Sew the different halves together to make two new blocks. Repeat with the remaining blocks from step 3 to make a total of 102 newly combined Nine Patch Variation blocks.

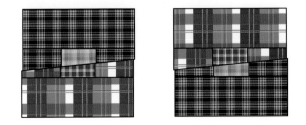

6. Trim the blocks to measure 6½" x 6½", angling them a bit as shown. Cut some of the blocks so they "tilt" left and some so they "tilt" right.

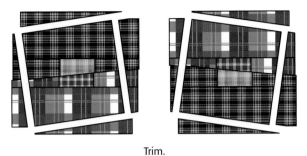

Trim.

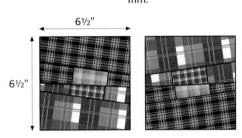

6½"

6½"

Make 2 (102 total).

> **TIP**
>
> If you layer and cut four blocks instead of two, you will have more possible combinations to sew together.

### Appliquéing the Letters

1. Refer to "Bias-Tube Letters" on page 21 and use the 1¼ yards of red fabric to cut 1⅜"-wide bias strips and make 7 yards of bias tube for letters.

2. Use a copy machine to enlarge the letters on page 51 as instructed. Referring to the quilt photo on page 47 and the quilt diagram on page 50, trace the words *Just Breathe* onto the 18½" x 60½" blue strip. Use uppercase and lowercase letters. Do not worry about perfection. The letters benefit from their charming freehand style. Complete alphabets, both uppercase and lowercase, are provided on pages 52–53 if you prefer to create your own message. You may need to enlarge or reduce the letters, depending upon your message.

3. Use a glue stick to secure the bias tube to the marked background to create the letters. Turn under the raw edges at the ends of the tubes and appliqué the letters in place with a whipstitch and matching thread.

## ASSEMBLING THE QUILT

1. Arrange the Nine Patch Variation blocks and the lettered background in horizontal rows as shown in the quilt diagram below.

2. Sew the 12 blocks above the lettered rectangle together to make a row; press. The center seams of the blocks will not match. That's what gives the Nine Patch Variation blocks their wonderfully fun "whopper-jawed" or askew look.

3. Sew the three blocks on either side of the lettered rectangle into vertical rows. Make two rows. Sew these rows to the left and right sides of the rectangle; press.

4. Sew the remaining blocks together to make seven horizontal rows. (Again, the center seams of the blocks will not match.) Press the seams as shown.

5. Sew the rows from steps 2, 3, and 4 together to complete the quilt top. Press the seams toward the lettered row.

6. Layer the quilt top with batting and backing; baste. Quilt as desired. Use the 2"-wide bluish green strips to bind the quilt edges, and label your quilt.

Quilt diagram

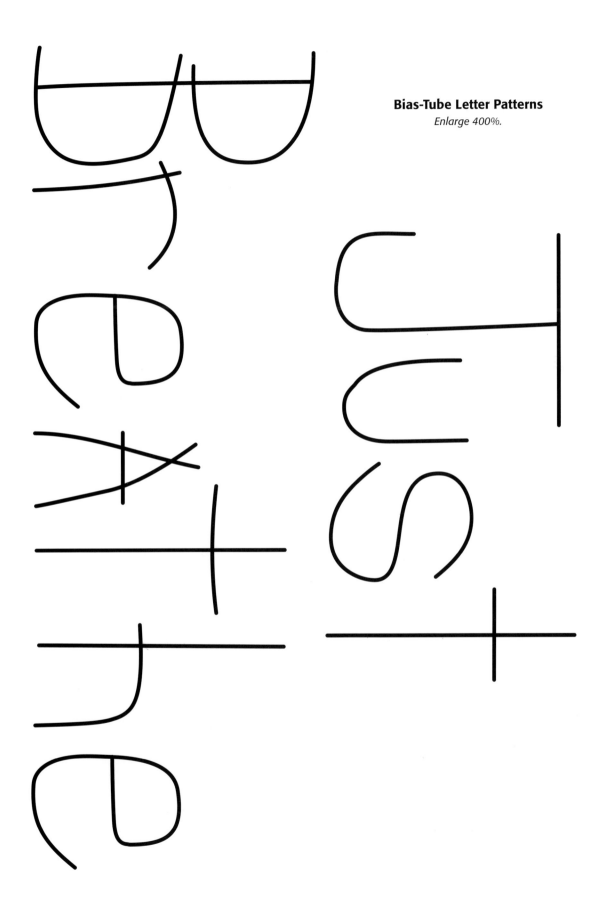

**Bias-Tube Letter Patterns**
*Enlarge 400%.*

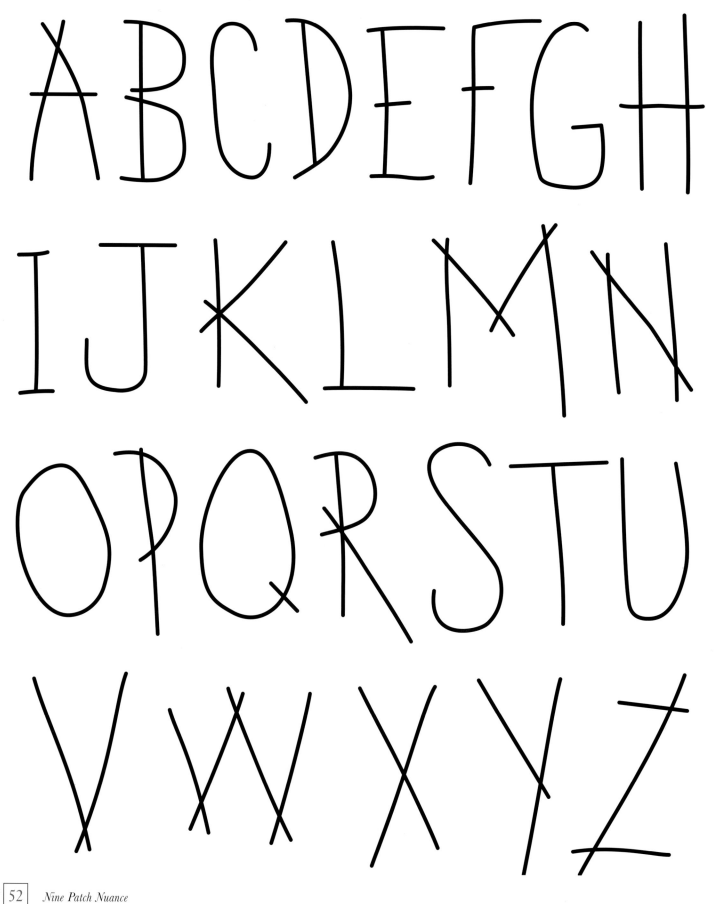

**Bias-Tube Letter Patterns**
**Lowercase Alphabet**
*Adjust size as needed for your message.*

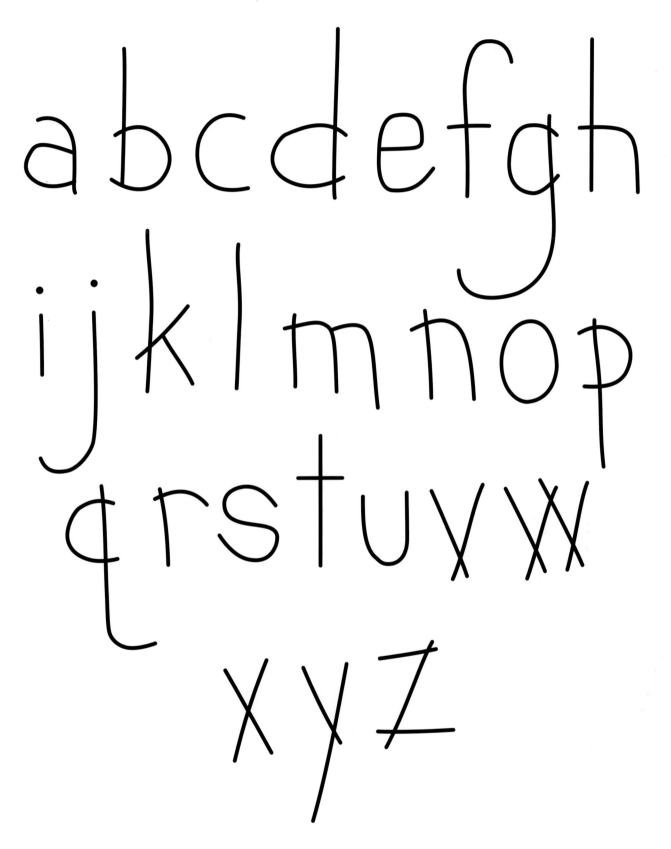

By Sandy Bonsib, 85½" x 105½". Machine quilted by Kathy Staley.

# FABRIC REQUIREMENTS AND SUPPLIES

*Yardage is based on 42"-wide fabric. Fabrics for piecing are listed from largest to smallest quantity.*

5 yards of red fabric for Pinwheel block A, alternate blocks, and border

3 yards of black fabric for Pinwheel block B and alternate blocks

2 squares, 6" x 6", of 32 assorted fabrics for Pinwheel blocks

1½ yards of red-and-white plaid for binding

8 yards of fabric for backing (horizontal seams)

92" x 112" piece of batting

## CUTTING

*Measurements include ¼"-wide seam allowances. Cut strips from the crosswise grain of the fabric unless noted otherwise.*

**From the black fabric, cut:**

6 strips, 6" x 42"; crosscut into 36 squares, 6" x 6"

6 strips, 10½" x 42"; crosscut into 17 squares, 10½" x 10½"

**From the red fabric, cut:**

5 strips, 6" x 42"; crosscut into 28 squares, 6" x 6"

5 strips, 10½" x 42"; crosscut into 14 squares, 10½" x 10½"

2 strips, 8" x 90½"*

2 strips, 8" x 85½"*

**From the red-and-white plaid, cut:**

2"-wide bias strips to equal 400"

*Cut these strips from the lengthwise grain of the fabric (parallel to the selvage).*

# MAKING THE QUILT

Refer to "Basic Quiltmaking Techniques" (pages 17–23) and "Finishing the Quilt" (pages 25–31) as needed. You will make 32 Pinwheel blocks. Each block is made from two fabrics. Eighteen blocks are made from two 6" matching print squares and the same black background (block A). Fourteen blocks are made from two 6" matching print squares and the same red background (block B). The finished blocks measure 10" x 10" in the quilt (10½" x 10½" unfinished).

1. Refer to "Two for One" on page 20 and pair one 6" assorted square with one 6" black square to make two half-square-triangle units; press. Use the same fabrics to make two more identical half-square-triangle units. Use a Bias Square® ruler to trim the units to 5½" x 5½".

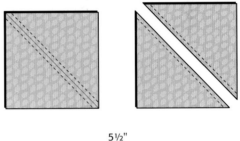

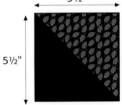

2. Arrange the four half-square-triangle units from step 1 as shown. Sew the units into rows; press. Sew the rows together; press.

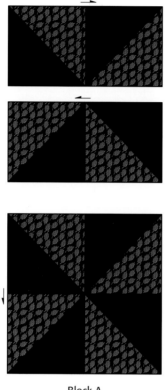

Block A
Make 18.

3. Repeat steps 1 and 2 to make a total of 18 blocks. Label them block A.

4. Repeat steps 1 and 2 using 6" matching assorted squares and 6" red squares. Make sure to trim the half-square-triangle units to 5½" x 5½". Make a total of 14 blocks. Label them block B.

Block B
Make 14.

## ASSEMBLING THE QUILT

1. Arrange Pinwheel blocks A and B, the 10½" red squares, and the 10½" black squares in nine horizontal rows of seven blocks each as shown in the quilt diagram below.

Quilt diagram

2. Sew the blocks together into rows. Press the seams away from the Pinwheel blocks.

3. Sew the rows together; press.

4. Refer to "Adding Borders" on page 25. Mark, pin, and sew the 8" x 90½" borders to the sides of the quilt. Press the seams toward the borders. Repeat to mark, pin, and sew the 8" x 85½" borders to the top and bottom of the quilt; press.

5. Layer the quilt top with batting and backing; baste. Quilt as desired. Use the 2"-wide red-and-white plaid bias strips to bind the quilt edges, and label your quilt.

By Sandy Bonsib, 85¼" x 85¼". Machine quilted by Kathy Staley.

## FABRIC REQUIREMENTS AND SUPPLIES

*Yardage is based on 42"-wide fabric. Fabrics for piecing are listed from largest to smallest quantity.*

3 yards of bluish violet fabric for fourth border

⅜ yard *each* of green, red, yellow, purple, gold, blue #1, pink, and blue #2 fabrics for blocks

1⅛ yards of blue fabric for third border

1 yard of red fabric for first border

⅞ yard of black fabric for side and corner triangles

⅜ yard of yellow fabric for second border

⅝ yard of black-and-purple stripe for binding

5¼ yards of fabric for backing

92" x 92" piece of batting

## CUTTING

*Measurements include ¼"-wide seam allowances. Cut these strips from the crosswise grain of the fabric.*

**From *each* ⅜ yard green, red, yellow, purple, gold, blue #1, pink, and blue #2 fabric, cut:**

2 strips, 3½" x 42"; crosscut into 12 squares, 3½" x 3½". You will use only part of the second strip. Cut the remaining piece to 2" x 36".

**From the black fabric, cut:**

3 squares, 11½" x 11½". Cut each square in half on both diagonals to make 12 quarter-square side triangles.

1 square, 12½" x 12½". Cut each square in half on the diagonal to make 2 half-square corner triangles.

1 square, 7½" x 7½". Cut each square in half on the diagonal to make 2 half-square corner triangles.

**From the red fabric, cut:**

5 strips, 5½" x 42"

**From the yellow fabric, cut:**

6 strips, 1¼" x 42"

**From the blue fabric, cut:**

6 strips, 6" x 42"

**From the bluish violet fabric, cut:**

8 strips, 11¾" x 42"

**From the black-and-purple stripe, cut:**

9 strips, 2" x 42"

## MAKING THE QUILT

Refer to "Basic Quiltmaking Techniques" (pages 17–23) and "Finishing the Quilt" (pages 25–31) as needed. You will make 32 Four Patch blocks in four different color combinations. The finished blocks measure 6" x 6" in the quilt (6½" x 6½" unfinished).

1. Sew the 2" x 36" strips together in the following pairs to make strip sets as shown: green and red, yellow and purple, gold and blue #1, and pink and blue #2. Press the seams toward the darker fabrics. Cut 16 segments, 2" wide, from each strip set.

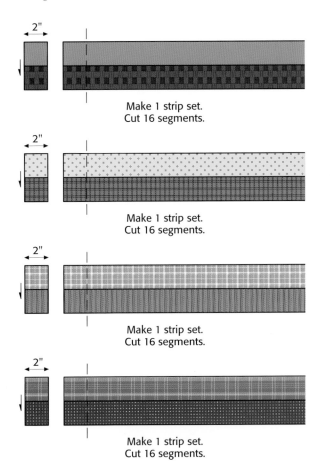

Make 1 strip set.
Cut 16 segments.

Make 1 strip set.
Cut 16 segments.

Make 1 strip set.
Cut 16 segments.

Make 1 strip set.
Cut 16 segments.

2. Arrange and sew two matching segments from step 1 together to make a four-patch unit as shown; press. Repeat to make eight four-patch units in each color combination (32 total).

Make 8 of each.

3. Arrange and sew a green-and-red four-patch unit, two 3½" green squares, and a 3½" red square to make a Four Patch Variation block as shown; press. Be sure to rotate the four-patch unit so that the colors create a diagonal line of two small squares and a large square. Make four.

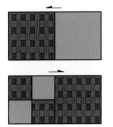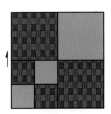

Make 4.

4. Arrange and sew a green-and-red four-patch unit, a 3½" green square, and two 3½" red squares to make a Four Patch Variation block as shown; press. Make four.

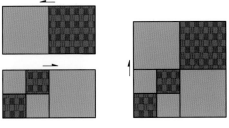

Make 4.

5. Repeat steps 3 and 4 using the yellow and purple four-patch units and 3½" squares, the gold and blue #1 four-patch units and 3½" squares, and the pink and blue #2 four-patch units and 3½" squares as shown. Make four of each variation.

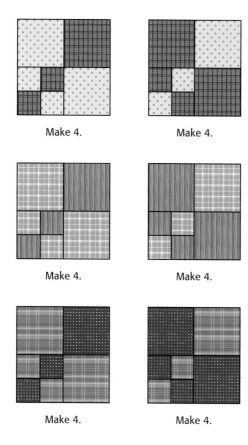

Make 4.  Make 4.

Make 4.  Make 4.

Make 4.  Make 4.

## ASSEMBLING THE QUILT

1. Arrange the blocks on point in diagonal rows, carefully placing the colors as shown in the quilt diagram above right. Place the black side and corner triangles. Note that the four corner triangles are two different sizes.

2. Sew the blocks and side triangles together in diagonal rows. Press the seams in alternating directions from row to row. Sew the rows together; press. Add the corner triangles last, pressing the seams toward the corner triangles.

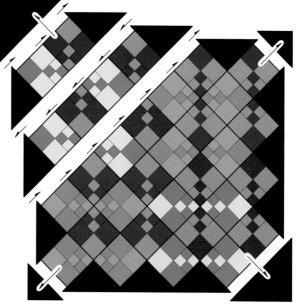

Quilt diagram

3. Trim the edges of the quilt top 1¼" from the corners of the blocks as shown.

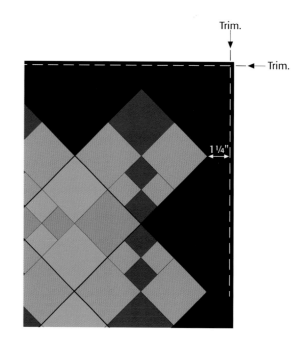

Trim.

Trim.

1¼"

4. Refer to "Adding Borders" on page 25. Trim two 5½"-wide red strips to 5½" x 40¼". Sew these strips to the sides of the quilt. Press the seams toward the borders. Sew the remaining 5½"-wide red strips end to end to create one long strip. From this strip, cut two 5½" x 50¼" strips. Sew these strips to the top and bottom of the quilt; press.

5. Sew the 1¼"-wide yellow strips together end to end to create one long strip. From this strip, cut two 1¼" x 50¼" strips for the side borders and two 1¼" x 51¾" strips for the top and bottom borders. Sew the borders to the sides, top, and bottom of the quilt as in step 4. Press the seams toward the new border.

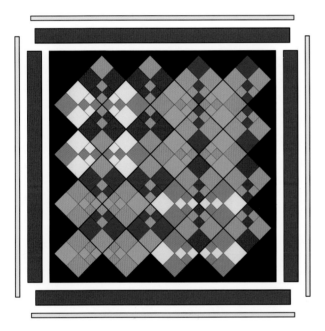

6. Sew the 6"-wide blue strips together end to end to create one long strip. From this strip, cut two 6" x 51¾" strips for the side borders and two 6" x 62¾" strips for the top and bottom borders. Sew the borders to the sides, top, and bottom of the quilt as in step 4. Press the seams toward the new border.

7. Sew the 11¾"-wide bluish violet strips together end to end to create one long strip. From this strip, cut two 11¾" x 62¾" strips for the side borders and two 11¾" x 85¼" strips for the top and bottom borders. Sew the borders to the sides, top, and bottom of the quilt as in step 4. Press the seams toward the new border.

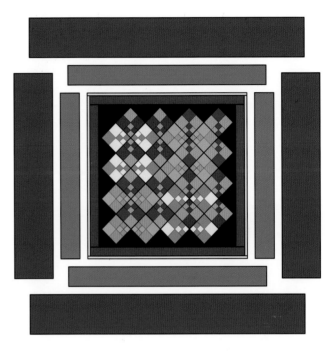

8. Layer the quilt top with batting and backing; baste. Quilt as desired. Use the 2"-wide black-and-purple stripe strips to bind the quilt edges, and label your quilt.

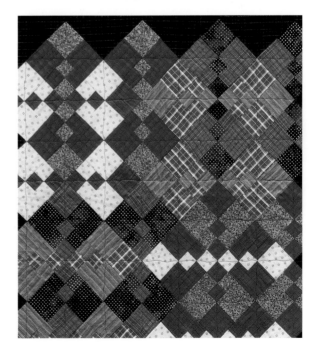

By Sandy Bonsib, 57¾" x 71½". Machine quilted by Kathy Staley.

## FABRIC REQUIREMENTS

"Bear's Paw Bonanza" is a scrappy quilt and you can include a wide variety of prints, plaids, stripes, and checks in the fabric mix. With so many different fabrics, it is difficult to tell you the exact number of fabrics, the amount of any one fabric, and the exact total you will need. When an *assortment* is indicated, the amount given is only a guideline. You can mix ¼-yard cuts (9" x 42"), fat quarters (18" x 21"), ⅛-yard cuts, and large scraps, depending upon how scrappy you want *your* quilt to be. You may work with fabric from your existing fabric collection, with fabric purchased specifically for this quilt, or with a combination of the two. You may wish to add fabrics as you go along. If you are purchasing ¼-yard cuts, fat quarters, or ⅛-yard cuts, you will be purchasing more than the totals listed in order to have more variety to choose from. Read through all the instructions before you begin.

## MATERIALS

*Yardage is based on 42"-wide fabric. Fabrics for piecing are listed from largest to smallest quantity.*

3 yards *total* of assorted fabrics for paw units (fabric A)

3 yards *total* of assorted fabrics for paw-unit backgrounds (fabric B)

2 yards of purple plaid for border and binding

1 yard of black fabric for side and corner triangles

3⅔ yards of fabric for backing (horizontal seam)

63" x 78" piece of batting

## CUTTING

*Measurements include ¼"-wide seam allowances. Cut strips from the crosswise grain of the fabric.*

### From the assorted A fabrics, cut a *total* of:

328 squares, 2⅛" x 2⅛", in matching sets of 4

82 squares, 3¾" x 3¾"*

*Cut one square to match each set of 2⅛" fabric A squares.*

### From the assorted B fabrics, cut a *total* of:

410 squares, 2⅛" x 2⅛", in matching sets of 5

### From the black fabric, cut:

7 squares, 10" x 10"; cut 5 squares in half on both diagonals to make 20 quarter-square side triangles. Cut the remaining squares in half on the diagonal to make 4 half-square corner triangles.

### From the purple plaid, cut:

6 strips, 8" x 42"

7 strips, 2" x 42"

## MAKING THE QUILT

Refer to "Basic Quiltmaking Techniques" (pages 17–23) and "Finishing the Quilt" (pages 25–31) as needed.

### *Making the Paw Units*

You will make 82 paw units. Each unit is made from two contrasting fabrics: one each of fabric A and fabric B. Refer to the unit diagram as needed. The finished units measure 4⅞" x 4⅞" in the quilt (5⅜" x 5⅜" unfinished).

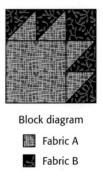

Block diagram
▦ Fabric A
◤ Fabric B

1. Refer to "Sew and Flip" on page 20 and pair one 2⅛" fabric A square and one 2⅛" fabric B square to make a half-square-triangle unit; press. Make four matching half-square-triangle units.

Make 4.

2. Arrange and sew two half-square-triangle units from step 1 and the remaining matching 2⅛" fabric B square together as shown; press.

3. Sew the remaining half-square-triangle units from step 1 together as shown; press.

4. Sew the unit from step 3 to the matching 3¾" fabric A square as shown; press.

5. Sew the unit from step 2 to the unit from step 4 as shown; press.

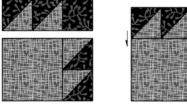

Make 82.

6. Repeat steps 1–5 to make a total of 82 paw units.

### *Making the Bear's Paw Blocks*

You will make 18 blocks. Each block is made from four paw units. The finished blocks measure 9¾" x 9¾" in the quilt (10¼" x 10¼" unfinished).

Arrange and sew four paw units together as shown; press. Make 18 Bear's Paw blocks. You will have 10 leftover paw units, which you will use to assemble the quilt.

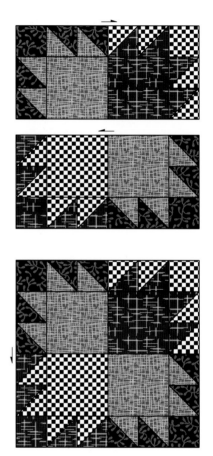

Make 18.

## ASSEMBLING THE QUILT

1. Sew a black side triangle to two sides of each leftover paw unit as shown; press. Make 10.

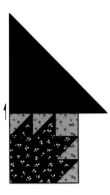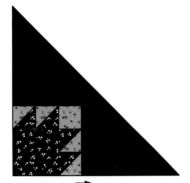

Make 10.

2. Arrange the Bear's Paw blocks on point in diagonal rows as shown in the quilt diagram below. Place the pieced paw side triangles and the black corner triangles. Balance eye-catching patterns, light and dark fabrics, and bright colors.

3. Sew the blocks and side triangles together in diagonal rows. Press the seams in alternating directions from row to row. Sew the rows together; press. Add the corner triangles last, pressing the seams toward the corner triangles.

Quilt diagram

4. Trim the edges of the quilt top 1" from the corners of the blocks as shown.

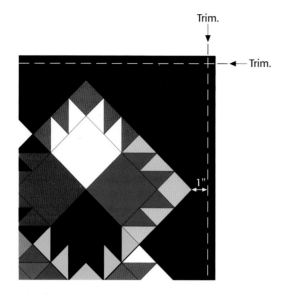

5. Refer to "Adding Borders" on page 25. Sew the 8"-wide purple strips end to end to create one long strip. From this strip, cut two 8" x 56½" strips. Sew these strips to the sides of the quilt. Press the seams toward the borders. Then cut two 8" x 57¼" strips. Sew these strips to the top and bottom of the quilt; press.

6. Layer the quilt top with batting and backing; baste. Quilt as desired. Use the 2"-wide purple plaid strips to bind the quilt edges, and label your quilt.

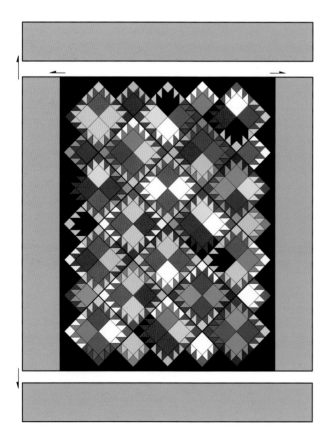

By Sandy Bonsib, 66½" x 88½". Machine quilted by Kathy Staley.

## Fabric Requirements and Supplies

"Rail Fence Riot" is a scrappy quilt and you can include a wide variety of prints, plaids, stripes, and checks in the fabric mix. With so many different fabrics, it is difficult to tell you the exact number of fabrics, the amount of any one fabric, and the exact total you will need. When an *assortment* is indicated, the amount given is only a guideline. You can mix ¼-yard cuts (9" x 42") and ⅛-yard cuts depending upon how scrappy you want *your* quilt to be. You may work with fabric from your existing fabric collection, with fabric purchased specifically for this quilt, or with a combination of the two. You may wish to add fabrics as you go along. If you are purchasing ¼-yard cuts or ⅛-yard cuts, you will be purchasing more than the totals listed in order to have more variety to choose from. Read through all the instructions before you begin.

## Materials

*Yardage is based on 42"-wide fabric. Fabrics for piecing are listed from largest to smallest quantity.*

12¼ yards *total* of assorted fabrics for blocks

⅔ yard of multicolored stripe for binding

6 yards of fabric for backing (horizontal seams)

72" x 94" piece of batting

## Cutting

*Measurements include ¼"-wide seam allowances. Cut strips from the crosswise grain of the fabric.*

**From the assorted fabrics, cut a *total* of:**

288 strips, 1½" x 42"

**From the multicolored stripe, cut:**

9 strips, 2" x 42"

## Making the Quilt

Refer to "Basic Quiltmaking Techniques" (pages 17–23) and "Finishing the Quilt" (pages 25–31) as needed. You will make 48 Rail Fence blocks. The finished blocks measure 11" x 11" in the quilt (11½" x 11½" unfinished).

1. Arrange six 1½" x 42" assorted strips in order from light to dark as shown. Sew the strips together to make a strip set. Press the seams toward the darker strips. Make 48 strip sets. Cut four 6½"-wide segments from each strip set (192 total).

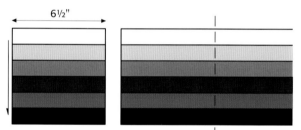

Make 48 strip sets.
Cut 4 segments from each strip set (192 total).

2. Arrange and sew four matching segments from step 1 in one of the combinations shown. Make a total of 48 blocks in any mix of the three combinations as desired.

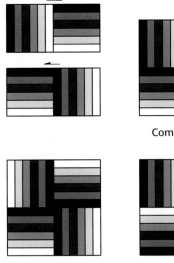
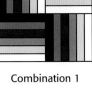

Combination 1

Combination 2          Combination 3

Make 48 blocks total.

3. Refer to "Two for One" on page 20. Layer two Rail Fence blocks right sides together and draw a diagonal line on the wrong side of the lighter block. Sew ¼" from the drawn line on both sides. Cut on the drawn line. Press each unit open. Each pair of blocks yields two Rail Fence half-square-triangle blocks. Make 48 blocks. Trim the blocks to 11½" x 11½".

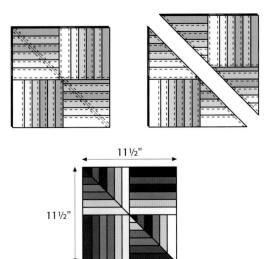

11½"

11½"

Make 48.

## ASSEMBLING THE QUILT

1. Arrange the blocks in eight horizontal rows of six blocks each, carefully turning the blocks as shown in the quilt diagram below.

Quilt diagram

2. Sew the blocks together into rows; press.
3. Sew the rows together; press.
4. Layer the quilt top with batting and backing; baste. Quilt as desired. Use the 2"-wide multicolored stripe strips to bind the quilt edges, and label your quilt.

By Sandy Bonsib, 64½" x 64½". Machine quilted by Kathy Staley.

## FABRIC REQUIREMENTS AND SUPPLIES

*Yardage is based on 42"-wide fabric. Fabrics for piecing are listed from largest to smallest quantity.*

4¼ yards total of assorted neutral fabrics for blocks*

2 squares, 5½" x 5½", of 14 assorted red fabrics for blocks (28 squares total)

2 squares, 5½" x 5½", of 9 assorted gold fabrics for blocks (18 squares total)

2 squares, 5½" x 5½", of 8 assorted blue fabrics for blocks (16 squares total)

2 squares, 5½" x 5½", of 8 assorted black fabrics for blocks (16 squares total)

2 squares, 5½" x 5½", of 5 assorted pink fabrics for blocks (10 squares total)

2 squares, 5½" x 5½", of 5 assorted orange fabrics for blocks (10 squares total)

2 squares, 5½" x 5½", of 4 assorted green fabrics for blocks (8 squares total)

2 squares, 5½" x 5½", of 4 assorted blue-green fabrics for blocks (8 squares total)

2 squares, 5½" x 5½", of 4 assorted blue-violet fabrics for blocks (8 squares total)

2 squares, 5½" x 5½", of 4 assorted violet fabrics for blocks (8 squares total)

½ yard of black-and-gold check for binding

4 yards of fabric for backing

70" x 70" piece of batting

*Pieces must measure at least 6½" x 6½".*

## CUTTING

*Measurements include a ¼"-wide seam allowance. Cut strips from the crosswise grain of the fabric.*

**From the assorted neutrals, cut a *total* of:**

128 squares, 6½" x 6½"

**From the black-and-gold check, cut:**

8 strips, 2" x 42"

## MAKING THE QUILT

Refer to "Basic Quiltmaking Techniques" (pages 17–23) and "Finishing the Quilt" (pages 25–31) as needed. You will make 128 scrappy Flying Geese Variation blocks. The finished blocks measure 4" x 8" in the quilt (4½" x 8½" unfinished). You will have one 5½" pink square and one 5½" red square left over. Set these aside for another project.

1. Refer to "Two for One" on page 20 and pair two 6½" assorted neutral squares to make two half-square-triangle units. Repeat to make a total of 128 half-square-triangle units. Use a Bias Square ruler to trim the units to 5½" x 5½". *Trimming to size is very important.* See "Squaring Up the Blocks" on page 22.

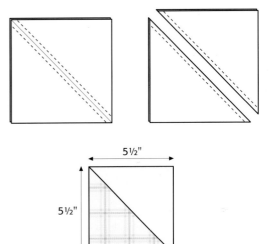

Make 128.

2. Referring again to "Two for One," pair one half-square-triangle unit from step 1 and one 5½" colored square to make two half-square-triangle units. Mark on the wrong side of the colored square. You may need to use a light pencil for darker fabrics. Repeat to make 256 half-square-triangle units. Use a Bias Square ruler to trim the units to 4½" x 4½", taking care to align the diagonal marking on the ruler with the short center seam on the unit as shown. *Trimming to size is very important.*

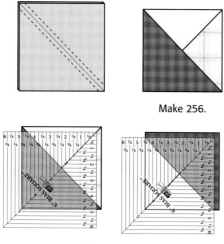

Make 256.

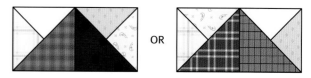

Trim to 4½" x 4½".

3. Sew two different pink half-square-triangle units from step 2 together as shown. Do not press yet. Make six. You will have six pink half-square-triangle units left over. Reserve these for step 5.

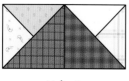

Make 6.

4. Sew two different red half-square-triangle units from step 2 together as shown. Do not press

yet. Make 24. You will have six red half-square-triangle units left over. Reserve these for step 5.

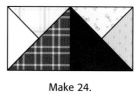

Make 24.

5. Sew one leftover pink half-square-triangle unit from step 3 and one leftover red half-square-triangle unit from step 4 together as shown. Do not press yet. Make six.

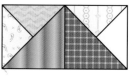

Make 6.

6. Sew two different orange half-square-triangle units from step 2 together as shown. Do not press yet. Make 10.

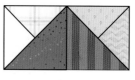

Make 10.

7. Sew two different gold half-square-triangle units from step 2 together as shown. Do not press yet. Make 18.

Make 18.

8. Sew two different green half-square-triangle units from step 2 together as shown. Do not press yet. Make eight.

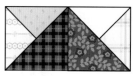

Make 8.

9. Sew two different blue-green half-square-triangle units from step 2 together as shown. Do not press yet. Make eight.

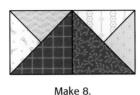

Make 8.

10. Sew two different blue half-square-triangle units from step 2 together as shown. Do not press yet. Make 16.

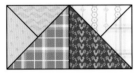

Make 16.

11. Sew two different blue-violet half-square-triangle units from step 2 together as shown. Do not press yet. Make eight.

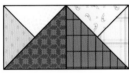

Make 8.

12. Sew two different violet half-square-triangle units from step 2 together as shown. Do not press yet. Make eight.

Make 8.

13. Sew two different black half-square-triangle units from step 2 together as shown. Do not press yet. Make 16.

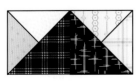

Make 16.

## ASSEMBLING THE QUILT

1. Arrange the blocks in a spiral as shown in the quilt photo on page 70 and the quilt diagram below. Start in the center of the quilt with the pink blocks and rotate clockwise as shown, moving on to the pink-and-red, red, orange, gold, green, blue-green, blue, blue-violet, violet, and black blocks. When you have finished arranging the blocks, press the block seams in alternating directions from block to block.

2. Sew the blocks together in horizontal rows as shown, pressing the seams in alternating directions from row to row. Note that you will need to sew some of the blocks together in pairs first in order to complete the row. Pay careful attention to the order and orientation of the blocks as you sew them together.

Quilt diagram

3. Sew the rows together; press.

4. Layer the quilt top with batting and backing; baste. Quilt as desired. Use the 2"-wide black-and-gold check strips to bind the quilt edges, and label your quilt.

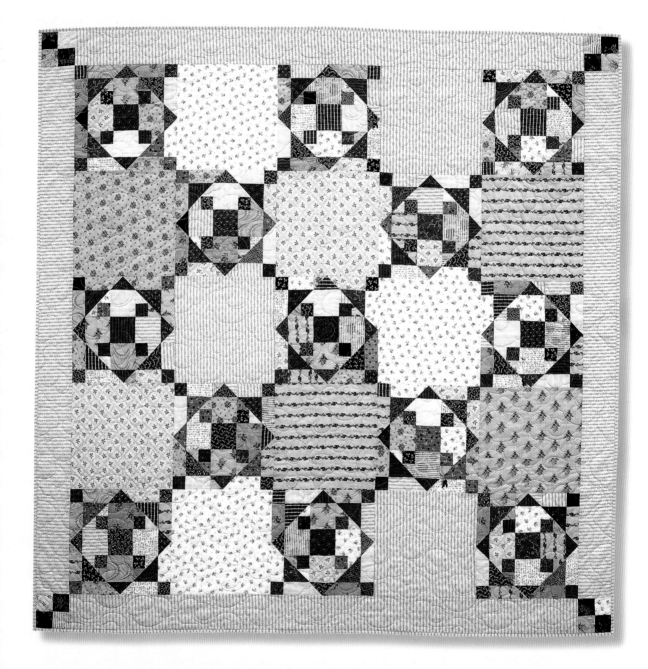

By Rachel Vanderlaan, 68½" x 68½". Machine quilted by Kathryn Milburn.

## FABRIC REQUIREMENTS AND SUPPLIES

"Sierra's Sunshine and Stars" is a scrappy quilt and you can include a wide variety of prints, plaids, stripes, and checks in the fabric mix. With so many different fabrics, it is difficult to tell you the exact number of fabrics, the amount of any one fabric, and the exact total you will need. When an *assortment* is indicated, the amount given is only a guideline. You can mix ¼-yard cuts (9" x 42"), fat quarters (18" x 21"), ⅛-yard cuts, and large scraps, depending upon how scrappy you want *your* quilt to be. You may work with fabric from your existing fabric collection, with fabric purchased specifically for this quilt, or with a combination of the two. You may wish to add fabrics as you go along. If you are purchasing ¼-yard cuts, fat quarters, or ⅛-yard cuts, you will be purchasing more than the totals listed in order to have more variety to choose from. Read through all the instructions before you begin.

## MATERIALS

*Yardage is based on 42"-wide fabric. Fabrics for piecing are listed from largest to smallest quantity.*

3¼ yards *total* of assorted light and medium-light fabrics for blocks, alternate blocks, and corner blocks

2⅜ yards of medium fabric for borders and binding

1½ yards *total* of medium and medium-dark fabrics for blocks, alternate blocks, and corner blocks

4½ yards of fabric for backing

75" x 75" piece of batting

## CUTTING

*Measurements include ¼"-wide seam allowances. Cut strips on the crosswise grain of the fabric unless noted otherwise.*

### From the assorted light and medium-light fabrics, cut a *total* of:

104 rectangles, 2" x 3½" (A)

52 squares, 3½" x 3½" (B)

104 squares, 2" x 2" (C)

52 squares, 2⅜" x 2⅜"; cut each square in half on the diagonal to make 104 half-square triangles (D).

12 squares, 12½" x 12½"

8 squares, 2½" x 2½"

### From the assorted medium and medium-dark fabrics, cut a *total* of:

52 squares, 2" x 2" (E)

52 rectangles, 2" x 3½" (F)

26 squares, 3⅞" x 3⅞"; cut each square in half on the diagonal to make 52 half-square triangles (G).

13 squares, 3½" x 3½" (H)

52 squares, 2" x 2" (I)

8 squares, 2½" x 2½"

### From the medium border and binding print, cut:

4 strips, 4½" x 60½"*

8 strips, 2" x 42"

*Cut these strips from the lengthwise grain of the fabric (parallel to the selvage).*

## MAKING THE QUILT

Refer to "Basic Quiltmaking Techniques" (pages 17–23) and "Finishing the Quilt" (pages 25–31) as needed. You will make 13 scrappy Sunshine and Shadows blocks. The finished blocks measure 12" x 12" in the quilt (12½" x 12½" unfinished). Refer to the block diagram as needed.

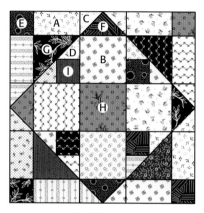

Block diagram

1. Sew two D triangles to one 2" I square as shown; press. Make 52.

Make 52.

2. Sew one G triangle to each unit from step 1; press. Make 52.

Make 52.

3. Refer to "Sew and Flip" on page 20 and sew two 2" C squares to one 2" x 3½" F rectangle as shown; press. Make 52.

Make 52.

4. Arrange eight 2" x 3½" A rectangles, four 3½" B squares, four units from step 2, four units from step 3, four 2" E squares, and one 3½" H square as shown. Sew the pieces and units together in rows; press. Sew the rows together; press. Make 13 blocks.

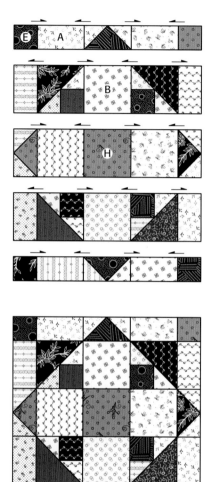

Make 13.

## ASSEMBLING THE QUILT

1. Arrange the Sunshine and Stars blocks and 12½" x 12½" alternate blocks in five horizontal rows of five blocks each as shown in the quilt diagram on page 77.

2. Sew the blocks together in rows. Press the seams away from the pieced blocks.

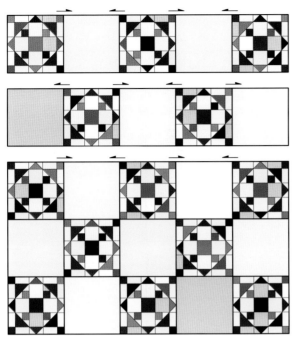

Quilt diagram

3. Sew the rows together; press.

4. Referring to "Adding Borders" on page 25, mark, pin, and sew a 4½" x 60½" border strip to opposite sides of the quilt. Press the seams toward the borders.

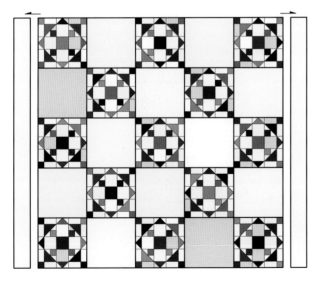

5. Sew a 2½" light or medium-light square to a 2½" medium or medium-dark square as shown; press. Make eight. Arrange and sew the units together as shown; press. Make four.

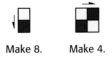

Make 8.     Make 4.

6. Sew a corner block from step 5 to opposite ends of each remaining 4½" x 60½" border strip as shown, noting the position of the light and dark squares; press.

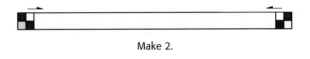

Make 2.

7. Sew the borders to the top and bottom of the quilt top; press.

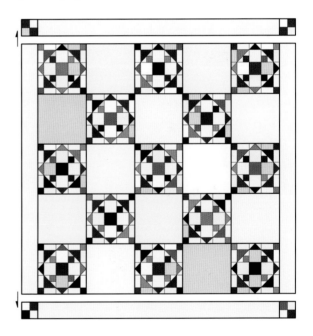

8. Layer the quilt top with batting and backing; baste. Quilt as desired. Use the 2"-wide medium fabric strips to bind the quilt edges, and label your quilt.

Sandy Bonsib is a teacher by profession and a quilter by passion. She has a graduate degree in education and has taught locally since 1993 and nationally since 1997. This is her seventh book. She has appeared on *Lap Quilting with Georgia Bonesteel*, *Simply Quilts* with Alex Anderson, and was one of six featured artists on *Quilts of the Northwest, 1998*. Through In The Beginning Fabrics, a quilt shop in Seattle, Sandy coordinates Quilts for the Children, a group that makes quilts for the children of battered women.

Sandy lives on a small farm on Cougar Mountain in Issaquah, Washington, with her family and many animals. She also raises puppies for Guide Dogs for the Blind.

For information about Sandy's classes and lectures, consult her Web site: www.sandybonsib.com.